The Code
of Traditional
Archery

Walking The Path...The Legacy of
Traditional Bowhunting

Grant Richardson

Primitive Stone Archery - Scouting -Tracking Inc. Publishing

The Code of Traditional Archery

Walking the path... The legacy of Traditional Bowhunting

Edited by Jerry Gowins

ISBN 978-1-7389080-0-4 Paperback

First Paperback Edition

Contents

"To my Ancestors who walked before me with Stick & String...

May the tradition continue in the fields and forests for future generations"

- Grant Richardson

For my grandfather, who taught me to walk with, talk to, and listen to the wildlife & the land.

For my father, who showed me I had my own path to find & walk in the forests, to find the circle of life our ancestors pursued.

- "In the Pine & Poplar"

And for my children, who renewed in me the magic reflected in their eyes, of the same wild places I discovered so many years ago. Thank you.

Forward

By E. Donnall Thomas Jr.
Author of Traditional Bows and
Wild Places & Longbow Country

The world seems awash in outdoor writing these days, and in my former position as Co-Editor of *Traditional Bowhunter Magazine*, I saw a lot of it. The quality of the prose varied wildly, and the subject matter ranged from a rehash of what had already been said many times before to material that would be of little interest to our readers. Nothing made me happier than to receive fresh and original material from a contributor I'd never heard from before.

That last sentence succinctly describes Grant Richardson's new book, *The Code of Traditional Archery*. It may be easiest to begin by explaining what this book is *not*: a tally of trophy animals, a "how-to" text as boring as a bad college lecture. Granted, he does discuss some traditional archery practicalities, but in a way that I found thoughtful and intriguing even after shooting traditional bows for 70 years.

In my favourite chapter, he recounts the introduction to bowhunting that he provided his young daughter. In addition to serving as a useful roadmap for others teaching their children about the outdoors, it is just a darn good read. Those familiar with the process—past, present, or future—or who maintain fond memories of a similar upbringing in their own past, will be delighted.

An Ontario native, Richardson, comes from a family well-steeped in the traditions of the bow, and his respect for some of the greats who preceded us all flow throughout.

I highly recommend it to anyone who currently accepts the challenge of hunting with a traditional bow or hopes to in the future.

Don Thomas - Lewistown, Montana

Introduction

Born Into Tradition

I was born into a family where hunting was an old-world pursuit full of tradition. Tradition. You will see that topic come up a lot in this dialogue, for those very traditions are the drivers behind a skill set that has taught me resiliency and fortitude.

My late grandfather and father provided me with not only direction but enough rope to have me learn my own path and the mistakes that came with that process. My grandfather, being a Conservation Officer with Fish & Wildlife Ontario, was very old school in his approach to teaching. Direct immersion into the skillsets was his method, and he taught me how to track and scout wildlife and other bushcraft skills.

In my early years, I learned what nature had to teach me. If you are a student of the woods, it's education through failure, trials, and hard knocks. I was raised to respect the outdoors and be responsible for learning about ecosystems. I was not allowed to hunt alone for upland birds or waterfowl with a firearm for almost three years after getting my hunting license. My father always allowed me to take my bow, however. He said that if you really want to learn how to hunt, grab your bow. As a result, I spent most of my free time in my early years chasing game after school and on weekends. When hunting seasons closed, I fixed my sights on fly fishing and flinging arrows with my father and uncle Bruce, who taught me that "roving" in the woods and fields was an important part of shooting for hunting scenarios with a bow and arrow. I listened intently to their stories of failure and success, devoured books and articles on the subject, and read all of Zane Grey's novels on the wilds of North America and the west.

I often came home empty-handed in my youth, but the lessons in the woods and uplands of those years led me to experience a much more intimate connection to those wild spaces. *Success was more than just accuracy with a bow.* Learning to be a hunter and a woodsman was equally, if not more important.

Getting close was the key. To get close, knowledge and an appreciation of the process were critical. The end state was not success but rather the experiences and nuances that hunting with the bow brought forth. With my bow, I chased rabbits, grouse, Hungarian partridge, pheasant, even ducks and geese, and the holy grail of my youth, the whitetail deer. I lost arrows, of course, in the process and occasionally connected, learning the hard way that the bow was a primitive weapon, an art form of silence, patience, and tenacity. It forced me into becoming a hunter and not just a shooter. The bow demands discipline and consistency. It proves its lethality when used correctly and appropriately, delivering an arrow to the intended target. Its purpose is ancient and effective. Without the employment of sights, scopes, or mechanical aids, the arrow went where I was looking. I am older now; I have been using a stickbow to hunt for almost 40 years.

It still teaches me something about myself every time I enter the woods, whether I pull back the string and let an arrow fly or not. For it is in that moment when the limbs bend to my input and vision of where the arrow will go that I make the decision to release the arrow with ethics and stewardship well in hand. More importantly, it connects me to my ancestors and ancient hunter-gatherers who beckon me to the forest and field to hunt with them.

I teach my children the same ways, to scout, track, and hunt with archery equipment but, most importantly, to respect the limitations of traditional archery's platform. A good teacher understands the student's needs and can build on what he/she already knows. At that point, the actual journey begins in developing their path of connection to our ancestors.

If ethics and the stewardship accompanying it are the backbones of The Code of Traditional Archery, the lessons learned therein are their foundation. It may be argued that every human alive on earth today can trace their existence to hunting by their ancestors as a means of sustenance and survival. Hunter or not, meeting this head-on will help you to understand our crucial connection to the earth. It will resonate within you a desire to protect her. More than ever, it is critical to understand this connection at the core of who we are and our resiliency as a species.

My hope for you, the reader, is that you connect with your roots. You may not come from a family of hunters, but at one point, your ancestors did forage, farm, and hunt. It is how they survived and thrived in an environment that very few of us will ever experience in our time. It is a part of us all and crosses all races and cultures. At some point, we all found our food in much the same way and faced that challenge as a natural process.

I am a firm believer in walking the way of the traditional hunter, in every sense of what that means; a woodsman, tracker, and conservationist, as well as having the ability to bring true free-range food home to the table. This "lessons learned" book contains parts of my path and process from my walks in the woods and fields. I hope it will guide you to seek your own path and tread with a newfound respect for the wild places you encounter.

If you are reading this book, you may also be walking the path of the hunter-gatherers who came before us. Or maybe, you want to try hunting with a stick and a string for the first time.

Herein you will find the code of traditional archery.

I invite you to walk with me.

Chapter One

Primitive Process

The Drive to Hunt

There are approximately three million bowhunters across the United States and many more in Canada. A predominance of these hunters shoot a compound bow. Now, I am not averse to compound bows or technology and, in fact, encourage folks to get into the woods and hunt in the manner that suits them ethically and is sound within the laws of the province or state they hunt in. I am more averse to how some folks use hunting equipment outside its intended scope of effectiveness and purpose. That use is not so much a challenge as is oft stated, but more so the ego talking, leading down the path of unethical behavior. There are a number of those bowhunters that use what is called "Traditional Bowhunting" equipment, or "trad" as it is often called these days.

When I began to shoot a bow in my childhood and into my teens, there was no traditional archery or trad bow hunting; it was just bow hunting. It was known as a close-range intimate way of hunting quietly. Compound bows had started to gain a lot of ground and popularity.

My romance began at that age with what folks nowadays call stickbows. The lure of compound bows and their wheels, cams, and cables just did not appeal to me like the lines and curves of laminated wood. There is a soul in a recurve or longbow. In that handcrafted bow is the heart of a craftsman, a bowyer who had put their hands and heart to work on crafting that bow. The bowyer pays close attention to intricate details and the precision effort of limb designs and profiles.

A passion is forged within its wooden design, one that will connect anyone who opens themselves to the process, whether hunting with a bow or target shooting. That soul I speak of is imparted from the bowyer while he or she is aware of the weapon's job and the performance necessary to be built into it. Finally, tillering the bow to craft it into something that connects to a part of me, I now realize is an ancient part of who we all are as hunter-gatherers.

The Code of Traditional Archery and bowhunting espouses three pillars that connect in a process that grows as one progresses on this path of hunting. This evolution when hunting with a stick and string is very personal and will be familiar to anyone reading this book who has already walked with a bow in hand.

Hunting the hard way by relying on a much more primitive method stokes a fire from within. That very pursuit involves preparation, planning, and knowledge of both the connection to that and the habits of the wildlife and environment in which they live. It is the process that matters more than the taking of game animals. That process is the driver for pursuing wild game with a simple wood bow and arrow.

The process can be broken down into three pillars of what my Code of Traditional Bowhunting has evolved into a method for myself:

1. Weapons proficiency and shot accuracy, the kinetic and kinaesthetic process of shooting a bow effectively for hunting purposes.

2. Ethics to guide us on our journey to ensure effective shot presentations and to be part of the circle of life connecting us with our past.

3. Conservation and stewardship of the environment and connection to the predator/prey cycle that we as hunters understand in a way that is intimately connected to our wild spaces. Unless they have walked this path of the hunter, many will not grasp this connection. If you choose to walk this path, it will spur you to become a fierce defender of the wildlife, woods, fields, and waterways we hunt.

Ethics plays a large part in this process and is the true litmus test of anyone who hunts, as the approach one uses to pursue the game and choose when not to take a shot or not is more important than releasing the string. Once the arrow is loosed, it cannot be recalled.

Traditional bowhunting has become popular again. The surge it has created has resulted in eliminating gadgets added to a simple process and the notion that a traditional bow is a "struggle stick" or a novelty weapon that is somehow tedious to use and less effective than other forms of hunting. Adding to something simple is, at times, a quick fix. In other words, falling back on gadgets to make you a better shot compensates for putting the time in to develop good shooting habits, etc.

I can argue that becoming a better shot faster is efficient, but the problem is that we have gone into a space of needing everything quickly.

I call it the "vending machine syndrome." Put in your money and expect results. Don't get results and, "bing," frustration begins; blame the weapon first, then blame the method when the process is not going fast enough.

Like anything done correctly, that requires effort. Traditional bowhunting is a process with a necessary foundation. Taught from the beginning, this process will improve in time as experience is gained.

A shooter trains for a shot process based on targets and the 3D range, which is fine; it is an aspect of making archery a year-long pursuit. Being a good "shooter" has become the priority instead of becoming a good "hunter" with a traditional bow.

The problem occurs when one shoots on a target range or 3D course and believes they can make the same shot on a wild animal. This is not the case. Ranges and, for the most part, 3D courses are often set up with challenging shots that are unethical and farther than most people could shoot under actual hunting conditions rather than a sanitized comfortable 3D shoot. Sure, the pressure to perform in front of your peers is there, but I dare say the most critical pressure on anyone chasing game with any bow and arrow should be to place that arrow in the animal ethically and reasonably to enact a quick kill.

This process is developmental with traditional bowhunting. Success is the driver but never a guaranteed result, and this process does not end but ebbs and flows with success and failure being tied together.

This issue has been exacerbated by an industry that pushes the same notions of the traditional bow being slow, that speed matters, etc., and that technology is more ethical.

In fact, nothing could be further from the truth. Archery seasons from their inception were longer because getting close and being effective was difficult, and harvest rates were much lower than firearms. Industry and its champions would have you believe that without a $300 rangefinder, binoculars, and the latest sights and release aid, you have no chance of hitting anything consistently. I routinely see folks shooting out to almost 100 yards on targets, and while this certainly shows capability with the weapon, it essentially trains folks to get good at shooting at foam animals. The problem is that foam does not move! In setting the distance bar farther and farther away, we are also setting the ethics of bowhunting farther and farther away from the purpose of the original archery seasons. In other words, the farther away the goalpost is moved, the farther away ethics is moved as well. I do not care what weapon one hunts with, compound, crossbow, or rifle, but I tend to be very rigid when it comes to staying within the ethical and lethal boundaries that each weapon's platform demands.

Stretching the "arrow," so to speak, in distance will most certainly stretch the capabilities and risk of shooting at a live game animal that does move! I once helped a gentleman quite some time ago who had transitioned from a compound to a recurve and was having issues. He had purchased a very pricey custom recurve from one of the top custom makers of bows. He could not understand why he was having problems being accurate at even 20 yards after shooting a compound for all the years he had. Among other things, he had presumed that the bow would do the work for him. He said he was having as he said, "target panic" and would find it difficult to hold the anchor point and would shake and lose focus. It was indeed a beautiful, well-built bow, but it was simply too heavy for him to handle effectively. Notice I use the word "effectively." He could draw and shoot five to six arrows before tiring. He had been using a release aid over the past nine years while shooting a compound and had used very little of what is called 'back tension,' those back muscles needed to assist in the drawing process.

Consequently, he had almost zero back tension and raised the bow high in the air to draw after shooting only a few arrows. He was practically ripping the string back and was having issues where his compound would break over and "let off" a great deal of the draw-weight. Meanwhile, the recurve just kept getting more challenging to pull. Back tension involves using the archer's muscles in the shoulder blade area to effectively draw a bow instead of using just one's arm.

I introduced him to a lighter-weight recurve, had him go through a few shots, and shoot 10 yards from the target. After initiating these changes, he was amazed that all his arrows were sitting in a decent group. He was not getting tired and could manage the weight of drawing the bow and focusing more on his shot. As a result, he began to stop worrying about drawing the bow. We began to work on his consistency and developed an efficient shot that worked for him! You see, it was not the bow's fault. The expensive bow did not make him shoot any better; it was a great bow, but the input it received from him was not working. It was never the weapon; it was the operator. This process is accomplished through a micro, macro approach which develops consistency under real bow hunting structured shooting presentations to develop this cycle into a habit for the individual. Setting up a foundation for consistency comes from what is between your ears; you're sighting and kinesthetic systems are highly evolved and key to capturing what works with archery that combines hand-eye coordination with other archery-specific qualities.

Think of performance athletics; how does the quarterback receive the ball and, under pressure, throw that ball to the receiver? Not instinctive? Yes, it is, in the realm of how the ball is getting there in principle, but it took a considerable amount of training, no matter how "natural" it was for him to throw that ball well. Hand-eye coordination, kinesthetic and kinetic function, body mechanics, timing, focus, and correct placement all played a part. The ability to make that throw was broken down into smaller attributes and worked to a very high degree of performance through training and under pressure in scrimmages to make it functional. Macro and micro methods are how I also teach folks to shoot instinctively.

Train for the big picture, that of shooting the bow for results as a macro approach in developing the individual's foundation. We then work with a micro approach to individualize the attributes under varying degrees of pressure and difficulty to become functional in shooting for actual bow hunting situations, not the target's bullseye. Performance attribute training and good drills equal function. What is that quarterback sighting with? Not a clicker, not a scope, not a release, nor any gadgets or sights. Yet they can, at the National Football League level, throw almost seventy-plus yards with consistent accuracy under pressure with no mechanical aids!

A fly rod has no scope, yet people can accurately cast to a rising trout at distances up to fifty feet with a wind! They are not watching the fly rod; they are looking at the fish. In the same way, you are looking at the target with a bow and arrow, different platform, same delivery system.

My friend with the pricey bow ended up trading it back to the bowyer for a lighter weight and longer recurve the following week. When I saw him again a month later, he was shooting realistic hunting-based shots at 20 yards or less with great consistency and accuracy.

Later that fall, he called me to help him track a whitetail buck he had shot at dark, which we found after a short thirty-minute tracking job. Funnily enough, even after cleanly taking that buck, he still stared at his bow and the deer back at the trucks that night, remarking, "I can't believe that little bow killed that deer." He had taken a whitetail deer with a stick and string. This was not the first time I had heard that same comment of disbelief from first-time stickbow hunters. He was experiencing a learning curve as a hunter and making a connection that night.

The process is what matters, and it is a difficult one. Time and time again, I drill that into folks; taking an animal with a weapons platform that is simple, effective, and, at the same time, not the easy route. If you are looking to improve your shooting ability or have always wanted to start shooting a recurve, longbow, or selfbow and have always worried about hunting with one effectively, read on.

The secret, if any, is to simply practice and put in the flight time. That is part of the formula for solving the "struggle stick mentality," the riddle of the "wood," so to speak. As shooting is a perishable skill, it requires maintenance. The bow forces this maintenance upon us to wield it with authority. If you intend to use a stickbow to hunt with, you should have that same authority in casting pointy sticks from it with unwavering confidence and without any thought of the weapon being a "struggle stick." No sights are needed, no unique set of instruments or other tech; the only route to being accurate is practice and time. Imagine if we sat behind the wheel of our vehicles each day with a "struggle car" mentality? Or a construction worker or tradesman called the tools they use daily "struggle tools?" In the absence of humor, the "user" or operator gives the device, tool, or vehicle function.

The "pain point" is there for sure when using a stickbow. The issue is that a lot of "good" practice will do far more for consistent accuracy using one's innate abilities than any shooting aids ever will. It is this aspect that folks seem to not want to connect with when picking up a recurve or longbow vs. a compound, so they install shortcuts and tech onto the bow to make it more efficient and easier to use.

Apart from the romance and simplicity of the wood and lines that attract many to traditional bows, within those very arcs, colors, and warmth lies the bow's ability to contain great power. By ancient design, the stored energy manifesting within the bow's limbs as it is drawn creates a fusion between the user and weapon that binds us to the fabric of the tool itself. The individual's skill, ability, and intent merge as one with the bow, and the operator connects with an understanding that what they are using requires skills to maintain effectiveness.

Maybe you have never hunted or even shot a bow or have hunted with a crossbow or compound and want to switch over. Perhaps you want to connect to a process that is older, ancient, and primitive. Herein, you will read how I stumbled and walked on. It is a constant learning process that I am still refining to this day.

I have, in most cases, provided insights from lessons learned into how to effectively connect and give context to this process, as well as solve some common issues. I have opened the door; it is for you to walk through and make your path. Ultimately, you, the individual, will learn to apply these same principles to your methods since the individual is more important, and his/her own flight time is the teacher and guide. In this realm of understanding, I hope to set you forth on your path in the fields and mountains of the world to connect with that inner hunter and inspire others to do so as well.

As they say, if it were easy, everyone would be doing it.

Chapter Two

Failure

The Path to Resilience

It was a gray day. A light snow had been falling, and the sun had been hiding behind the stratus formations for several days. It looked more like waves than clouds as large flocks of northern mallards beat against it while attempting to land in the slough that connected the river a mere 100 yards from where I sat. The old oak tree had been used by another bowhunter many years prior. I looked down at the creased and weathered 2x6 plywood I was standing on and wondered how long it had been nailed across the wedged branches. It was a "wolf" tree. It had used up almost all the nutrients of the surrounding vegetation and stood mountain-like on the lee of the hill, a shelter for roosting owls and porcupines, and my vantage point, almost 14 feet up its trunk.

Pulling the hooded grey wool sweater my grandmother had knit tighter around my chin, I shivered in the briskness of the afternoon. I had been waiting for one of the grouse that had come strutting out toward me as they often did late in the day.

I imagined slowly pulling the string of my recurve back before sending a turkey-fletched shaft at one of the bush chickens my grandfather exalted as "Pahtridge." Imagining was all I could do at that point, as I had no bow.

That was before I could carry a bow into the woods. Although, at 10 years of age I had followed my father around in the woods and waters since I was three, acting as both flusher and retriever for grouse, and rear paddler for jump-shooting ducks. This, though, was the passion that haunted my dreams; bowhunting.

Earlier that summer, while at a large outdoor shoot, I had met some other youth who had already been hunting in states that allowed archery youth seasons. I was supremely jealous of them. My bow lay in its case in the back of my father's truck, consisting of two pillowcases camouflaged with brown and green magic markers and stitched together with pieces of latigo and nylon backing from one of my fly reels. Midday, I was allowed to take my bow out and shoot in the sandpit with all the other hunters in that area, where they gathered to share tales of deer seen, not seen, and missed chances. Everyone had nicknames. Some, if not all, were relegated to a part of their persona or ability with a bow and arrow.

For me, traditional archery and bowhunting was just bowhunting. In those days, I had developed a romantic view of the recurve, with its laminations and curved faces sending

arrows with authority to their intended targets. My thoughts
went back to my father, who I had been deer hunting with
for the past two weeks of the season. A trained archeologist
and schoolteacher by trade, his time in the woods counted as
his church, where he alone conducted quiet sermons with the
woods and wildlife. These last few years were different for me
as he had begun to take me with him more and more, and
instead of having to pull at him when he arrived home from
a hunt for details, I was able to be present for this sacred part
of his life he now shared with me.

The area we were hunting was one of Ontario's first
archery-only bowhunting deer seasons at the time: a tree nurs-
ery spanning 1100 acres.

My father had been one of the individuals driving for
archery-only seasons in those days as President of the now-de-
funct Ontario Bowhunters Association.

Settled into my stand, I heard it; a snap like soft lightning
behind me, 70 yards up the rise on the short ridge where
my father was sitting in a large pine tree with his longbow.
I strained to listen to what sounded like branches snapping
far behind me, where I'd heard an arrow deflecting off a tree
moments earlier. Pausing, trying not to breathe, I heard only
the wings of the mallards whistling against the torrent above
my head. Silence fell, and the wind subsided as the evening
thermals gently swirled.

I sat there for almost a half-hour, wondering what had happened as I looked skyward at the skeins of waterfowl flying overhead. Had Dad shot a grouse? Or maybe a snowshoe hare? He wanted one for a stew. He'd told me so earlier that week. I was startled from my daydream by my father's voice an hour later. He was there in front of me, moving methodically and making no noise. He beckoned me to climb down and motioned for me to be quiet.

"I got a shot," he said, and my heart jumped. Dad got a shot!

My excitement at what had happened was stifled by the look on his face. I was bursting at the seams to find the deer, but his expression told a story that would unfold much later. It would be one of the most remarkable learning experiences that impacted me as an archer, traditional bowhunter, and woodsman.

Dad relayed what had happened. The scrape he had been sitting on had been visited by a large 8-point. He'd gotten off a shot, then saw the arrow deflect as it reached the deer. The sound I had heard was indeed the arrow careening into the woods. We found some white, if not sparse, hair at the shot location. The deer had bolted before slowing down. We started on the blood trail and found little blood. The arrow was nowhere to be found. We followed his track without much other sign at that point. The blood trail finally began 60 yards from the shot site.

My father was a meticulous tracker. It seemed like we had only gone a little way, which was taking a very long time.

"We need to back out and give him some time," he said. I was upset at this and began to worry. It did not make sense; Dad was a great shot! "He has taken deer before, and we have blood," I thought as we packed into our truck to head home.

That was the first blood trail I had been on alone with my dad. The week prior, he had been having me tag along more since he saw more deer with me than without or with his hunting buddies. His superstition was proving correct.

After several hours at home, we returned and got on the blood trail again.

It was now midnight on a Sunday night, and while all my peers in school were sleeping for the next school day, I was out in the dark woods trailing a deer with my father. Driving back into the tote roads that night seemed ominous, and I recall feeling like my role of tagging along was suddenly elevated to another status.

The blood had been spotty from the start, and we soon found where the large deer had bedded down. It did not look good. There was little to no accumulation of blood where the buck had bedded, then arose and walked off in the light skiff of snow that had fallen the previous day. My father moved slowly, at times on his hands and knees, crawling, stopping, and signaling for me to tag sign. At times I had no idea what he wanted me to tag with the orange paper trail marking tape. But as we went on at a snail's pace, I realized that it was the actual track of the deer, a broken twig or leaf that had been stepped on, not just the buck's blood.

That was the start of a long night; the archery season was over the next day, and my father knew the woodlot would be full of gun hunters looking to fill their tags and likely walking all over the track. The snow on the ground was light. There were patches here and there as the buck track entered a swampy bedding area. We pushed our way through the dense cover of swamp maple, and tag alders combined with soft ground and tangles; we had to crawl for several yards at times, and I was growing tired, wet, and cold. My father pushed on slowly, ensuring he was still on the right track, as that was literally what we were following at the time. He would pause and check the trees as well.

It was now early morning. We had been on the buck's track for almost six hours, and as we crawled out of a pocket of alders into a small clearing, I looked up at the sky. In my hands was a tiny flashlight that my grandfather had given me. I held it up like a blazing torch to ward off the darkness. We stopped and sat for a moment; my mind thought of all my friends in their beds asleep. The wind bit at my face, and I began to feel for the first time that I was a part of something bigger than anything I had felt before. Time changed for me, and I realized somewhere deep down that I was a part of something far more ancient than I could have imagined.

My father turned to me, and I could see him slowly waving me forward to him in the ambient light. His face had changed, and he looked calm and centered. He sat down, kneeling in the snow, and somehow, I knew he wanted me to follow. We knelt together like we were giving credence and honor to the darkness and clouds swirling around the waning crescent moon above. He pointed with his finger and whispered for me to listen. I could see nothing and strained to hear in the blackness that now consumed us. I froze in place and could hear noises in the field ahead of us in the darkness. After what seemed like a half-hour, we edged into the clearing, and my father turned and waved for me to follow. We walked to the edge of a small field, and he shone his light across a large cutover of growing young maples. There, standing at the edge of the field, was the buck with three does. We watched them vanish like shadows into the opposite woodlot, the buck showing no signs of slowing down and looking fine as he cleared a tall fence with no signs of injury.

We took a large loop around the field to an adjoining road for the long trudge back to our truck. I looked up at my father and asked him if he thought the deer was fine.

"Yes," he said. "He was feeding along the apple trees on the fence there with the three does when we broke out of that alder swamp. We followed him through."

I was disheartened. Did dad know he hadn't made a good shot?

And why did we follow the deer for so long? From the beginning, he told me later as we walked out, he knew he had shot low and under the deer. Not only that, but the blood trail, or lack thereof, and white belly hair at the site where the shot was taken had told the same story; he had found the hair when he first looked before fetching me and thought he had shot under, to begin with. Nonetheless, he'd made a nonlethal hit, and he needed to ensure that the animal was not wounded and going to be lost.

I asked him why we followed it so far?

"I owed the deer that much. I shot and drew blood, and you don't give up until you are certain."

We chatted about the whole event, and I could tell he was disappointed. We had been out in cold weather and sat for hours waiting, only to get a shot and not recover the animal.

It had been as much about my education as a bowhunter as it was about finding the deer for him that cold night. Knowing that the deer would survive was some solace but spending that time with him that day and the following morning, going through what we did, brought us closer together as father and son. That aspect taught me to understand the difficulty the hunt truly brought; failure was the teacher, and my father was my guide. I had learned through failure that it isn't about success, and for the first time, I had been tracking an animal and using all the skills he and my grandfather had taught me up until that point in my life.

I connected with a part of my ancestors that night; the pursuit of food and the responsibility that comes with it. I had hardened my hunting resolve and grown, and I often reflect on what I would not have learned if it had been easy to partake in the learning experience in those moments of failure and hardship. That night opened my mind to the depth of the process of what success is measured by, and more importantly, the lessons that failure teaches us in connecting to our primal nature and facing those failures head-on in forging the iron in our souls to survive in adversity and our ancient resilience.

My father has been a grampa for over 20 years, allowing me room to teach my kids through my experiences in the woods and waterways. He still shoots his longbows weekly and mentors his grandkids. All his Grandkids have had bows given to them and arrows and quivers made, and they all shoot. Our youngest received her first hunting recurve this past Christmas and will be out chasing game with it this fall. She will experience her success and failures and forge her way in the crucible of nature, and I will celebrate them with her. Creating a legacy is critical for youth in our sport today.

Chapter Three

Close Encounters

Of the Antlered Kind

I had been waiting for almost two hours before he came home. My father and I had been planning on deer hunting behind an old dump adjacent to nearly 500 acres of Crown (government) land.

While hunting Hungarian partridge with my Springer spaniel earlier in September, I found a well-used deer run with rubs all along it. I was very excited; for weeks, I had been scouting and locating a spot to sit on a small oak ridge that bordered natural grass fields, cedar fence lines, and a tight cover swamp on the other side. One tree had a massive rub on it, and I was determined to bowhunt that area with my father. This was my second year bowhunting, and I had been watching the calendar with anticipation for opening day for weeks. That afternoon after we got our bows out and began the walk along the overgrown farmland and bush trail that was a little more than a few hundred yards behind the actual dump road. As we walked, we flushed several grouse feeding in the apple trees and grape vines.

My father laughingly said that we should have brought our shotguns instead of the bows.

As we were making our way around the fence line to the main field, he stopped and pointed to a large patch of exposed earth under a low-hanging maple branch. The soil had been tilled up, and clods of grass and dirt hung from a nearby brush. There was a strong musky odor. An enormous deer track was in the middle of the almost three feet wide patch of earth. It looked like a symbol left by the deer, a challenge that said, "I am here." I envisioned an elk-sized whitetail churning up the dirt and grass to let me know this was his territory. We proceeded across the field, being mindful of the wind direction. My father pointed to a rock and tree roughly 90 yards away and whispered that he would sit behind a fallen portion of the fence where a secondary crossing was evident from the trampled grass. Nodding, I wished him luck. I knew exactly where I wanted to sit and ached with anticipation at seeing the massive rub I had found earlier.

Walking slowly, I came to a group of trees close to the other rubs and found several small rubs and a scrape the size of the one I had seen moments earlier with my father.

I could not believe my luck. This was the place! I found two small cedar trees close to my height against which to frame myself and kneeled, cradling my bow across my lap.

After the woods settled down a bit and I had been sitting still and quiet for several minutes, I began to imagine the trail ahead and anticipated where a deer would emerge from the swamp to the sparsely treed ridge where I awaited.

Several grouse tempted me a short time later, but I declined to take a shot at them even though they were mere feet away at one point as they scampered about picking sumac berries and windfall apples. I heard a sound that I had not heard before. I heard it again, this time more pronounced, like someone with a kid's party toy making a low buzzing noise. The grouse seemed undisturbed, continuing their way across the rocks and out of sight.

A doe burst from the cover behind me some distance away and ran across the field, jumping the cedar fence I had crossed earlier, her white flag waving in the air.

Her back hair was raised; she seemed agitated. I thought the wind had been good for me, but maybe she had winded me and bolted from her cover.

I heard the noise again, much closer, along with hoof falls. A loud snort cut the air from the swamp to my left, and I strained through the screen of trees to see its source.

Shifting slightly, I leaned out; I could make out the shape of a deer's hind end slowly walking through the trees toward the trail in front of me.

My heart began to pound. I glanced at the tip of my arrow and the scalpel-sharp broadhead I had fussed over for the past week. I worried that it and the other five in my bow quiver were sharp enough. My father reminded me not to play with them too much lest I cut myself. I lost sight of the deer and wondered if it had smelled me.

As I carefully pivoted to look at where the animal had gone, another low grunt cut the air and a snort followed by a much louder grunt. I made out an outline of the deer 70 yards from me and reckoned that it could go by either my dad or me. The buck then lowered its head and viciously raked and pawed the earth. For several minutes I sat in awe as Buckzilla tore up the scrape and the nearby trees paying particular attention to a small pine tree to rub his brow tines. My heart felt as if it were going to drop out of my chest, and after what seemed like half an hour, he suddenly began to move, but I could not get a good look at him as he walked into the mess of scrub cedars to my left.

I began to tactically imagine where he would step out to prepare for the shot. I surmised it would be on the main trail out of that swamp, about 20 yards away, moving from left to right. I raised my bow. I could hear him walking closer to me. I could not believe it, and my anticipation became electric.

He stepped out a mere 14 feet away and turned to face a small wind-bitten pine. He then destroyed that tree as if he had a vendetta to settle with it. At that, all my confidence fled; he looked immense. I counted 12 points, six to a side, and his beams looked like a burr oak with long tines like tipped lances.

I could see his breath in the cold air, as he stepped out a mere 12 feet away. I pulled the string back and let the arrow fly to his heart, only to watch it fly hair-shaving close over his back. He jumped and stood looking where my arrow had deflected off a large stone several feet behind him. I ripped another arrow off my quiver and nocked it. As I raised my bow, the arrow clattered against the riser. He turned toward me as I drew and shot again. This time it missed as he leaped in the air. The great buck stopped and looked my way again, then bounded over the cedar fence and ran across the field in the direction the doe had taken earlier. I had lost sight of him, never seeing him again.

I stood and began to shake as adrenaline surged through me. I was angry and excited simultaneously, largely disappointed for missing a deer like that so close to me.

My father was sitting on a rock against some trees and stood as I walked up to him and whispered that I'd shot twice at the giant buck. I walked him over to where the events had unfolded; we found both arrows and he had me show him exactly where the deer had come in and where I was positioned when I shot. One arrow buried in a cedar tree after deflecting off a rock behind the buck. I debriefed my father on what had happened as I dug it out of the tree.

It was growing dark now, and clouds rolled in from the north, bringing flocks of ducks on the wind into the nearby swamp, like smoke billowing from the skies.

We found the buck's track. I told dad again I had cleanly missed. He looked at me and asked me to show him where the deer had jumped the fence. We followed the buck's track for nearly 800 yards across the field. The buck had walked right down the path used by the doe. There was no sign of injury. As we crossed the last cedar fence to the old tote road leading back to our car, we heard a loud snort-wheeze from the field to our left, then crashing and the sound of several running deer.

As dejected as I was on the ride home that night, something had stirred in me; a sense of accomplishment even though I had not hit the deer. I had been able to scout, locate and get close to a mature whitetail buck without him knowing I was there. I had the locate, scout, track and hunt part. Now all I needed to do was close the circle and connect, but why hadn't I? That question ultimately led to some soul-searching that resulted in stark clarity. The way I had been shooting and practicing was deficient.

I had not fired even one arrow from a seated position, and it had cost me my first deer. I was determined to correct this oversight.

I hadn't prepared for that shot, nor could I control my adrenal dump. I did not have target panic yet, but I was halfway there. I had shot at the whole animal and not focussed on correct shot placement. It had also been the very first time I had been around a big game animal in close proximity while actually hunting.

In my young mind, the buck from the cover photo of every magazine I had ever read growing up suddenly walked out in front of me and reality hit hard. I had fallen to the level of my training in those moments and although I had made two shots in succession at the buck, my inexperience and lack of hunting flight time in shooting structure for that scenario had exposed a gap I was determined to correct and build upon.

An easy way to develop correct shot placement is by studying an animal's anatomy and understanding where that arrow will enter *and* exit the animal. Get used to being around big game you are going to hunt. This exposure should be in videos at a minimum.

Watch and assess their behavior and where the vitals are located when moving.

Practice shooting from different positions; it is critical to shoot how you will hunt and maintain your follow-through!

Do not drop your bow arm to see where your arrow will hit. It is essential to remain focused until the arrow hits your mark.

Practice tactical breathing to control your adrenal state when an animal is coming in or is close. Inhale slowly for a four-count, hold for four and exhale slowly for a four-count. It is crucial to do so, even when you are practicing. It will become a habit and allow you to focus on where you want to place that arrow instead of shooting at the whole animal. Doing so will take flight time and experience, but you can do it with good training.

Find the arrow! Even when missing a shot, be certain you did not hit the animal. I have tracked and found several deer that archers thought they had missed altogether, but everything happened so fast amidst the excitement they did not realize they hit the deer. There is nothing like the feeling of scouting, preparing, arrowing, and recovering game after the effort put forth into the process. Embrace that feeling when it happens, slow down and savor it. The hunt is not over until you recover the animal.

I had learned through failure that it isn't about success, and for the first time, I had been tracking an animal while hunting and using all the skills he and my grandfather had taught me up until that point in my life.

It was time now, to connect those outliers and ultimately synthesize the hunter and the archer. The structure for the bowhunting game is not the same as target archery. Adding adverse but ethical shot presentations to your daily shooting will help you to evolve as a shooter and hunter in both form and function, embrace the challenge, put in the work and have fun!

Chapter Four

Connecting To The Hunter

The Rule of Three

We have many opportunities to succeed - and fail - in pursuing our quarry. These opportunities in which success happens are preceded by tremendous planning and effort in a process that continues long after a successful hunt.

The process and difficulty of hunting with a stick and string, the reality of being a competent bow hunter and not just a shooter, becomes relevant to anyone who has delved into this unique world of hunting close.

The earliest primitive weapons seasons, and the lengths of those seasons, centred around hunting with archery equipment. Success took time due to that difficulty.

I had several opportunities to hunt for deer that year. I was still in my teens and had the time that youth has to give to all without the responsibilities that adulthood brings. Time to drive to the woods, walk, sit, and hunt alone almost daily. I had blown several stalks that year and had begun to home in on some crucial lessons. Learning through hunting the hard way in the past few years, I had been able to bowhunt on my own for whitetail deer, the unicorn of my youth. My persistence had grown. No longer discouraged by failure but, in fact, fully embracing it, head on at times. Hunting had become a way of life, and that life began to bring forth strength and self-confidence that, at the time, was the dawn of my connecting with my resiliency as hunting does for those who genuinely step into the realm it offers.

Earlier that year, I snuck up on a mature buck only to fail to get a shot. The sneak took almost an hour to cross a small field. Although another deer across the next fence busted me, I had beaten the eyes and nose of a mature whitetail buck. I was only 10 yards away and preparing to shoot when the doe began to wheeze and blow at me. He sprang away, running a mere five feet from me at full pelt. I had gotten so close I could smell him.

I was headed to a well-known trail I found while grouse hunting in September with my bird-fevered Springer spaniel. It was a hidden area, an overgrown logging road cutover from a hundred years prior, now effectively camouflaged from its original purpose with tangles of grapevines, buckthorn, and blowdowns skirting a dried swamp. I'd already sat in front of the enormous oak three times that season; I preferred to switch it up between the two areas I was hunting that year, so I chose to walk into the dense cover of this hidden spot to hunt that day.

It had been a slow season; opening only two weeks earlier, it would close the next week and be open to rifle season.

I knew two crews would push the edges of the woodlot I was hunting that night, affecting the remainder of the season after archery opened again. I crept through a tangle of buckthorn and grapevines to get to the back of the old logging road, now overgrown and little more than a pathway lined by trees still weathering the effects of saws and axes long discarded. I was startled by a grouse taking off from one of the grapevines intertwined around a small cedar tree where it had been sitting, gorging on the frostbitten dark purple fruit hanging heavy in the afternoon sun.

I thought of my spaniel Erin and her happy tail wagging furiously whenever a bird took off from a flush. However, she was not with me, and the grouse banked high, giving a picture-perfect rising shot as it crested the tops of the grapevines, its brown phase feathers turning to brilliant copper as the rays of the sun warmly lit its rising flight.

This spot was special to me, a magical place I had discovered. I knew that no one had hunted it for a long time, likely due to the difficulty of bushwhacking to get to it. However, once inside the mess of bramble, the brush opened into two small overgrown clearings with two trails paralleling the opening. The centrepiece was an enormous, giant white oak that loomed like some ancient monument survivor of the clearcut that had occurred so many years ago. It stood defiantly with its long branches hanging down as if weary of being so magnificent.

The grouse had broken my focus, making me feel like my presence was now known to every creature inhabiting that quiet clearing. I had tried to sneak in like a shadow to the base of the oak, where I had the perfect area to sit, blending in at the base of the monolithic tree.

Back then, I would find a good spot, blend in, and kneel motionless; it worked for me and was an effective and flexible way to hunt. An hour had passed; I was watching a nuthatch crawl around a sapling in front of me, chasing out bugs from the tree's bark, when I heard what I thought was one of the grouse coming down the trail to my right. My eyes strained to see the source of the noise, now realizing it was most definitely a deer and not an old ruff walking toward me. Soon I could make out the shape of a deer paralleling the main trail that ran out in front of me.

I had already been busted at my other location two days prior. Worry began to creep into my mind as the evening thermals swirled around me and down the path, changing direction every few seconds.

I had my bow up at this point, my feet on pins and needles as I tried to adjust slowly for a better angle for the shot. I took several deep, slow breaths and focused on the animal as he made his way through the tangles. I knew the deer used the main run as had happened before, though they used it mainly at night, and the bucks seemed to be using the secondary trail that paralleled the main run. That trail was precisely where the buck was now walking.

The deer, now only 12 yards away and directly in front of my shooting lane, abruptly stopped and stared in my direction. Time slowed. I waited with the little 56-inch recurve in my hands. Breathing slowly, I focused on the deer's chest, not the antlers, which had fresh moss hanging off the brow tines. Looking for a gap, I picked a small area ahead of his path of travel. A cedar blowdown provided a foot-wide opening. He walked into the gap and began to turn away from me. I drew, hit my anchor point, and released in one fluid motion. The arrow disappeared as it reached his chest. He bolted, kicking up clods of mud and grass as he ran. It had happened in slow motion but, in reality, only lasted a few seconds. In those seconds of heart-beating stillness, the arrow had gone where I wanted it to. The crash I heard further into the woods told the story's end. I glanced at my watch and closed my eyes, forcing myself to stay still and focus on the sounds ahead of me in the thickness of the woods.

Standing slowly to let the pins and needles leave my feet, I took a deep breath and leaned against the old tree. I looked up at the branches, the sun fading onto the yellow leaves, now dry and brittle, some gently falling around me. I wondered how many wild dramas the tree had witnessed over the years between the weather and animals that had used it for shelter and collected its acorns in the 100-plus years it had been there.

Stepping forward after a half-hour of waiting, I walked gingerly to the path where the deer had been standing. I located the arrow, stuck firmly in a small cedar. The signs of a hit were evident. I tagged the tree with some orange trail tape, and, looking back down the path the arrow had travelled from the base of the tree, I focused on the hoof prints in the mud.

Picking my way slowly into the thick cedars, I crawled in and around many of the trees until it opened enough for clear sight into the fading light. There, only yards away, the buck was expired and serene against the forest floor. I sat down several feet away with my bow across my knees and gazed at him. At that moment, I don't know if I was awestruck by the knowledge that I had just taken my first deer or in disbelief that the bow had done what I knew it could do. Only now, it was at my hands, my connection to the animal and not someone else's. The intimacy of that moment struck me deeply, and I was in awe of the animal, feeling a reverence I had not fully experienced before. The process had now grown to include something else, caring for the meat and my heightened responsibility for the animal.

It dawned on me that I should get my father to share this experience. It was close to dark when we returned together to the fallen buck. We sat for several minutes in silence. After saying a word of thanks and dressing the deer, we began the drag out of the woods. My father and I spoke few words that night on the drag out. I insisted on doing all the work while my father accompanied me through the tangled fortress of brush and trees surrounding the opening where I had killed the buck. After a three-kilometre slog, which seemed to take hours, we finally arrived at the fence line and loaded the buck into the back of his pickup.

Catching my breath, I looked up at the shining stars. The wind had picked up a bit, and in the ambient light, I could see lines on my father's face that I hadn't noticed before. It was a moment of reflection that I will never forget. Something changed in me that day. After following him for years in the woods and waterways of my youth, something new had broken through; I was now walking beside, not behind, him. I had reached a new connection with my father to our ancestors. I now realize that in this connection of living and pursuing to hunt to live, I felt the resilience and self-reliance that has guided our species' survival over the time we have walked this earth.

My respect, admiration, and knowledge of the whitetail deer had also grown. My sense of protection for the ecosystem and the wildlife habituating it had grown fiercely. I now had a new appreciation and thankfulness for the deer in its life and habitat. To this very day, I have connected to our environment and the struggle all creatures experience and co-exist in nature because of hunting the hard way. The circle is constantly surrounding us as we go about our business in the concrete world we have created, whether we like it or not. This hunt was a hard-earned experience, not a given. Now I am teaching our youngest and am no longer in it for me. I am deeply immersed in helping to foster her traditions and creating those memories through her failures and success.

I have hunted in some archery-only areas in the US that required a shooting test before being able to proceed. Minimum weights are a requirement for reasons pertaining to ethical hunting. It is a generality that blankets certain species to ensure adequate killing efficiency.

Those laws are the driver for our ability to hunt with archery equipment; shoot whatever equipment you want but stay within the established limits. Whether you agree or not is beside the point.

Let's talk about that for a moment. As I have mentioned before, I have zero issues with whatever equipment folks hunt with as long as it's ethically sound. With the right effort and mechanisms in place, I can get most folks hunting-ready with a stickbow in 30 days, provided they follow the shooting platform and practices. They may be restricted to shooting at game from 10-15 yards away, which is where getting good at hunting and not just shooting comes into play. Your limitation with the bow should not limit how well you can learn to get close to your prey.

Walking out of the woods empty-handed is common. However, each walk should result in learning and improvement. I daresay the driver of hunting with a stick and string is more related to our innate connection with those who walked before us—those who had no other weapon of choice. No high-powered rifle and scope, no compound bow, nor the comfort of modern clothes and a warm vehicle to return to. Those are choices we all have available.

Either way, the idea of a simpler way of hunting and becoming effective in that method forces one down the path of history and a reckoning with one's modern self. It is within the process of deconstructing the modern hunter into something closer to our ancestors, a place we all came from, that we recognize a part of who we truly are. Limiting the hunting platform will quickly bring this to the forefront of your endeavors. It is a reliance not on technology, but ourselves, our instinct, our ability, and in the end, a traditional stickbow. It is more about the connection we have using a primitive weapon and how that weapon becomes a part of the ancient hunter we all are.

"Hunt close" is not just a term but rather an essential part of being a good bowhunter. The one obstacle I continually see is that many folks do not believe they can be good with the stickbow, or it can't be an effective weapon. As Yoda once retorted to Luke Skywalker (who, upon raising his x-wing fighter out of the swamp, says, "I don't believe it!"), "And that is why you fail." The same often rings true for folks when shooting a stickbow; the mental game, the struggle stick mentality, if you will, has in some cases ended up becoming an excuse for poor shooting rather than a driver to develop a strong connection to the bow.

Connecting and becoming effective with any process requires failure, the primary driver for pushing through and maintaining momentum in the face of adversity. I find that the finest bowhunters and woodsmen I have ever met failed many times and persevered to challenge themselves over and over to get to where they are now. They do not rush; they are slow and methodical and harness effectiveness in their manner and application, allowing them to see missteps and take corrective action.

I am often asked how much I practice shooting. My response surprises some people. Even after shooting regularly for forty-five years and hunting for thirty-eight years, I still shoot year-round. Archery, arguably for the most part with a stickbow, is, to a large extent, a perishable skill set that requires direct input to maintain. Allow me to explain. It is not just the quantity of shooting I do; it is the quality of training in my shooting. If I believe I have reached a certain point in my shooting, my ego will begin to take over, and I will start to plateau and stagnate since I will believe I have attained a high level of ability. The problem lies in that ability belief. If I am shooting at the same target, with the same three arrows at the same distance repetitively, then I am just getting good at that shot setup. That leads to complacency. It no longer challenges the brain, and growth ceases. You get good at shooting that target, distance and shot process. A "Groundhog Day" of shot practice, so to speak. To grow, you must challenge yourself. I am not talking about distances or obstructions like trees and rocks. I mean different positions and angles with good ethical shot presentations, just like in real hunting situations—shots you would either take or decline from taking.

I taught combative martial arts in the past, and coached MMA. When we held large seminars and training camps, we would not allow the students, regardless of rank, to wear belts. Mostly, there was no ranking system in what I was teaching. Your ability did the talking, not a belt. We could pick out the traditional clubs brown belts from the black belts almost every time. How? The brown belts were still hungry! They had not reached a point where they felt subconsciously, they had plateaued. They had the drive, would let it all out, and were still self-competitive! They were still growing.

Now throw BJJ (Brazilian Jiu-Jitsu) into the mix, and you see a different beast; a senior blue belt knows most of the submissions, positions, and defense a black belt does. But what does the black belt in BJJ have that the blue belt does not? Flight time! The black belt has more time in and has created, based on the same structure (base-position-control-defend-submit, etc.), and evolved their own application based on resistance training and rolling with many people of all sizes, ranks, and shapes and in competition with a fully resisting opponent.

What does all this have to do with traditional bowhunting? It is by adapting your shooting with your hunting skills, set up, and flight time attributes under pressure and isolating the individual pieces that make a shot work instinctively through training instead of practicing the same way at the same distance every time.

Folks that are doing trick shots isolate the trick shot. The result you see on social media has been isolated, practiced, and failed repeatedly. It is not training for bowhunting but training for a trick shot. While visually appealing, you will often notice a large, black background to make the target stand out for clarity so the archer can make the shot objectively. I'm not taking away from these amazing shots, but they are what they are, mastery of the trick shot.

If you isolate your process in what and how you are setting up your shots and not so much in how you are shooting your bow, you will find improvement much faster.

You will improve your shooting every session if you challenge your natural sighting system--the brain and hand-eye coordination that goes along with it--that is doing most of the work. It is one of the main reasons I do a lot of work on focus and focal point drills when I am shooting, not the standard three-arrow grouping often seen. I never want to lose that drive!

I use the rule of three to force changes in pressure; they are as follows.

Position. Always shoot from different positions (standing, kneeling, and seated).

Angle. Always change your shooting angles. Do not just shoot at broadside targets. Frequently change the angle at which you shoot the quartering away and broadside shots to burn them into your neural synapses. They are the primary high-percentage shots you want to take. If you train like you're going to hunt, your confidence will be there on autopilot.

Distance. Shoot within your effective distance, varying the distance with each shot. It will force your brain to adjust and compensate, and you will stop worrying about what the yardage is and focus much more on what's important- arrow placement!

Your mental game is crucial. If you feel lazy, your shot will be lazy; if you feel tired, it will reflect in your shooting. If you feel on point, confident, and alert, your shooting will reflect it. When you shoot at one distance every time, and random outliers occur while hunting, you will have difficulty compensating and will not rise to your expectations. You will fall to the level of your training.

Your mental game and the mojo you develop from the connection to your bow need to be as sharp as the broadhead on the end of your arrow; anything less, and you will question yourself under pressure. So, get in your flight time, switch your shots up and increase the difficulty within your effective lethal range. Add pressure and develop an application for good consistency that works for you! Remember this; you are only as good as your last shooting session. Everyone misses at one point or another. I have found that the miss has very little to do with one's equipment, but folks tinker and attempt to find fault with the gear, when it is just about more arrows down range.

One of the most challenging shots I have ever seen was by a fellow from Ontario who can shoot out a candle flame from 40 yards or more in a dark barn. He has developed a very consistent shooting structure and, in my opinion, is one of the finest instinctive archers I have ever seen, almost a Ronin of archery, if you will. Try that shot at a moving flame sometime at ten yards. It will help you adjust to just how important focus is when shooting and humble you at the same time. Take my word for it.

Remember, seeing those three arrows all connected in a group shooting from the same place each time makes the brain happy. It does not necessarily challenge it to grow. I want confidence in the folks I coach, not ego. Look at your process like honing a blade; the sharper the edge, the easier it will be to use, and a sharp knife is safer than a dull one. As the saying goes, If you give a man a fish, you feed him for a day. If you teach a man to fish, you feed him for a lifetime. I want to teach people to fish for themselves, not give them fish every day.

Break up your shooting specific to as many of your hunting situations as you can, and you will shoot better when the moment comes, and it really counts on a live game animal.

I have let down on three times as many animals as I have released an arrow at. This could be for many different reasons, such as the animal became nervous, maybe there was a branch or another obstruction, the animal turned and the shot was not there, another animal got in the way, etc. In these instances, I let down and waited for the right shot to present itself.

I am not in the business of coaching folks for Olympic archery, field archery, or even 3D championships. My aim (pardon the pun) is to show folks that anyone with the time, effort, and dedication can not only learn how to shoot effectively in a reasonable amount of time but be hunt-ready to pursue wild game with a bow, arrow, and one string, no matter who they are.

There is no guarantee with anything. Success is a matter of personal process and one's own experiences. For some, it is bringing home meat for the table. For others, it's just getting out to be in nature, and if it results in food, then all the better. For others, it is a way of communing, centering, and connecting with our past. In any regard and for whatever reason, this becomes an individual path. The lessons I learned all those years ago from that first deer have shaped into a memory of work and effort, which still resonates with me today.

Take your time to prep for the shot, control your breathing and focus on where you want that arrow to go. Focus is a hallmark of the shooting method I teach folks and is far more critical to making a shot on a game animal than picking a spot. A spot moves as the animal moves. Structure, in general, stays much more static unless the animal is running, and being able to focus on where that arrow is going to go is crucial. Without concentrated focus, you will have a hard time pointing your bow and sending that arrow where you are looking. Focal point drills will help this ability we all possess.

Shooting for the center mass of the shoulder crease is a common principle I teach folks in a hunt-ready accuracy course. Before and after you shoot, take some good, long deep breaths, (tactical breathing), in and out for the count of four. That will increase oxygen to your brain, assist your memory and calm the urge to get up and look immediately for the animal, which may cause serious issues in recovery if the animal has not yet expired. Wait! Slow down. It is not yet the time to cheer. Rarely does the animal drop within sight. Wait for a minimum of 30 minutes after the shot -- longer if you think you made a marginal hit. Focus on finding the arrow and mark the spot where you found it.

Ensure that you have control over your actions. In other words, do not rush into the trail. Take your time and go slowly. And as the saying goes, when in doubt, back out. And remember this; anyone who has hunted for any length of time has lost game. It happens to everyone! If someone claims they have never lost an animal, they were doing something else, not hunting.

The resilience of being immersed within the difficulty of relying on your ability with a stick and string in the wilds of our world will most certainly bring forth honesty and a stronger individual. Embodied in self-reliance, centered in the knowledge of what you are truly capable of, which in today's world, is a much-needed attribute.

Chapter Five

Immersion

Grandfathers Heritage

I learned the art of hunting when very young. My father's dad being an avid old-school outdoorsman influenced my appreciation for hunting from early on. "Slow down" was his motto, "you'll miss out on what's going on right in front of you." Many of the lessons I learned from him still resonate to this day.

I had 12 years of my young life with him until he passed on to the great hunting grounds. I am sure he casts for rising brook trout with a split cane flyrod and chases pheasants, grouse, and the beloved "timberdoodle," his favorite upland bird. He was from older stock and had many trades under his belt. He was an adept carpenter, welder, leather smith, jeweller, master gunsmith & decoy carver, winning several carving contests in both show and gunning categories. Apart from those pursuits, as a tracker and hunter, he was a Conservation Officer and Game Warden for several years in our province of Ontario. Decoy patterns, half-finished birds, and gunsmithing tools adorned his basement while the odor of cedar and basswood permeated the air of his shop. Sketches, stencils of decoy patterns and wildlife, and the required posters of dogs playing poker adorned the old shop's walls.

We spent most of our time outside that busy shop basement, walking just as the sun was rising. It was his favorite time of day.

"Fewer people about," he would say. "It gives us time to see things before they hide from sight from the rest of the world."

He had been walking that early fall with an old recurve my uncle had given him. "I need to get used to the weight," he told me, even though the bow was feather light.

I would get up quietly and amble my way down the stairs to his room, wake him up, and reach up for the book of North American birds he had sitting on his shelf. He would quiz me on different species and try to steer me away from upland bird color plates, often not successfully.

We would be out the door before anyone else. On this day, however, he was very intense and excited to show me something he refused to disclose to my eager pleadings.

In the early fall dawn, we walked down the path behind the house, stopping to quietly grab some raspberries before my grandmother woke to scold us for eating what few were left on the bushes. Crossing the barren highway, we stepped into the government land, a series of large overgrown natural grass fields with a spring-fed stream cutting through the middle and a beaver pond at the far end bordered by a large sandy area, then hardwoods.

As a child, my brother, cousins, and I roamed this area and often found broken pottery shards, arrowheads, and old tin pieces as this area had been a trading point nexus for the Huron Wendat First Nations peoples. It was precisely the kind of area a kid born into the outdoors could ask for.

He stopped at the edge of the hardwoods, which ran out into a small meadow, then to a short ridge that flowed into the fields. Kneeling, he pointed to a small oak tree that stood alone across the field some 100 yards away. "Stay in the shadows and watch that tree," he said while pointing to a large white oak with leaves beginning to turn to amber. After almost 40 minutes and my young brain growing restless, he pointed again and said nothing. The area behind the tree was moving as if the branches were breaking free. I strained to see what was causing the movement. Out stepped a large buck that had recently shed its velvet. We watched the deer picking up acorns for several minutes before he tapped me on my shoulder and beckoned me to follow. Into the scrub we went, walking slowly along the stream that cuts through the middle of the land. The stream was a distraction for me. Brook trout still resided there in certain parts where ancient upwells of cold springs brought respite to the vermiculated, white-finned haloed fish, and one could still catch them amidst the many creek chubs that resided there. I had seen my first wild ringneck pheasant there one morning while walking alone on the gravel road. The rooster strutted, picking at gravel before running off to hide in the tall grasses as I gave fruitless chase.

I snapped back to my senses as a branch whipped my face, instant karma for not paying attention to the lesson about to unfold inside the bush path. Once we were within 70 yards of the deer, he paused and beckoned me to kneel.

"Go get close to that deer," he said, not taking his eyes off the tree where the buck, still snatching acorns from the ground, was ambling about slowly. I stared at him, his silence answering me sternly without words.

I stood, bending low, and began to sneak by him. He grabbed my leg, "Stop!" and pointing at the grass bending with the wind, stated emphatically, "keep that grass bending toward you as you go to him."

I understood but doing so without being seen by the buck would prove difficult. I mostly crawled toward the deer, and when I popped up to get a better look, I saw the white flag of the buck running in great bounds back to the protection of the woodlot. I walked back to where my grandfather sat near the creek flipping crickets he had caught into the darkened waters.

"So, how did that go?" he said, not taking his eyes off the expectation of a rising trout to his terrestrial offerings.

"Not so good," I said. Grandfather laughed.

"Why say that? You got into easy rifle range. But if you want to fling arrows at them, you'll need to get into stone-throwing range. This is the deer's ground. He lives here, and you must learn what your ancestors did to get close to him."

He beckoned to the oak tree, "You know where he lives and eats. Now work on making the wind your friend. Oftentimes, she's a fickle foe, though." He said it with a warning tone and a smirk on his weathered face. I began to stand up.

"The last thing is to have a plan!" He raised himself up, and we began walking down the gravel road toward home.

Planning is of great importance. Equipment is just the beginning, and the shot process you choose is the bolt that holds the entire mechanism for success in place from a weapons perspective. It is yours alone to develop for the situations you will encounter with your single string.

The hunting piece though is the fabric of the entire process, and it is that very thing, that synchronous blending of hunting and shooting with a stick and string that demands much of the user. Unlike other forms of hunting which require little prep and practice (like modern firearms), traditional archery requires understanding the nuances of the type of bow, matching arrows, and of course the method of hunting you have immersed yourself in. This includes terrain, weather knowledge, and animals that inhabit the ecosystems in which you will pursue them. Much like the art of fly fishing, traditional archery requires you to develop an operating system that ultimately fits you and your tactics. One cannot walk into a store, grab a kit, and begin to fly cast and fish without some constraints.

Let's touch on that for a moment. The idea of a constraint means that there will be barriers to success by learning through failure. Developing a hardy way of sustaining oneself through this process involves understanding what we are truly capable of and facing down our ego simultaneously. Learning about the fly rod, line weights, how to cast, leaders, tippets, flies, etc. Developing the ability to read the water you're fishing and which flies to use. The presentation of said flies to the type of fish matters right down to the entomology of the water's ecosystem and holding areas. All that leads us to a process that is refined over time. The final analysis is to choose the fly to cast to the fish. The same goes for the bow in getting the arrow to the desired target with accuracy. That analysis becomes critical when pursuing game with a stick and string. It separates the archer from the bowhunter, and it will cause you much introspection along the way.

The steps in between, the preparation, weigh heavily in the principles of learning how to hunt close. This component to success is, at times, a steep ascent. It is inevitable that the teaching vector never stops, and that growth never ceases. Being adequately prepared will give you an intimate knowledge of your equipment and how it functions. That will help you adapt and evolve, refining your equipment's effectiveness in real-time situations with confidence and without hesitation.

I had the week off to hunt and had been sitting daily in a stand situated near a large creek. It was a classic wetland riparian habitat and an excellent stand for hunting the runs the deer used to navigate through the dense cover connecting that area to the higher uplands south of my location. It was an area only approachable by canoe. I slipped into the water, taking care not to let the limb tips of my recurve slap into the thwarts, and began to paddle quietly to my destination.

The sun was high in the sky by midday, but I had time to paddle quietly up the former glacial run-off that was now a beaver creek. I slipped the weathered green canoe across the old beaver dam, avoiding a sizeable chunk in its center from a breach in its mass of sticks and mud.

Surprised from its afternoon hunt across the dam, a mink stood on its haunches. It watched me paddle through the gap in the dam mere feet away, looking like a sleek brown statue in the sunlight. I slid the old Sears canoe into the reeds and, when close enough, quietly hopped to a log.

A flight of Blue-winged teal suddenly buzzed my head. I watched them navigate the upper reaches like a fighter squadron on a mission, twisting in mid-air, showcasing the sky-blue patches on their wings. I wondered where they had been a couple of weeks earlier when I'd hunted the pond they were pitching into upstream.

Being careful not to move too quickly, I picked my way to the edge of the woods and noted several deer tracks leading toward my stand. It was an easy walk, slightly uphill, and one I had mastered over the years of hunting here. Today though, I had a sense of urgency. The creek and pond would soon freeze as the forecast called for consistent below-zero temperatures and snow, making the route impassable.

The inclement weather arrived, forcing me to change my tactics. After an hour of high winds, the tree stand felt like a ship about to keel in a storm. I climbed down to still hunt the nearby open areas surrounded by tall stands of cedars adorning the nearby fence lines hoping to encounter some whitetails.

Although I had stalked this area prior and knew the terrain well, the wind messed with this decision as it blew north to northwest dispersing my scent into the main bedding area and adjacent deer runs. The area tempted the senses as it slowly rose into upland habitat. It broke into openings encircled with remnant apple trees growing wild from the once-cultivated farmland nearby. Its old cedar fences, now hanging low and overgrown with young maples, provided plenty of food and cover for whitetails.

The trails that crisscrossed its landscape stood out like deer highways, and the sight of fresh tracks and scrapes I encountered as I snuck into the openings made my heart beat faster.

I noticed the buck and his does immediately, However, I did not have a doe tag, and he was the first buck I'd seen that season.

He stood against the skyline near a half-fallen fence rail and was silhouetted by the low-hanging clouds as he slowly fed his way along the rise he was cresting. The fact that he was trailing four does, and the wind direction made this plan problematic. The flat, open terrain with sparse trees was an additional obstacle to getting within arrow range. Under the circumstances, five sets of eyes and noses would be challenging to defeat. I began to devise a plan to stalk him.

My strategy would require some bold moves. I knew the prevailing wind was coming across the field and to my left. I watched them as they browsed for several minutes, one older solo doe was the maven of this bunch, and she was checking her back and the wind constantly. After a half hour of watching them pop slowly in and out of the edge of the heavy cover, I put my strategy into action.

I opted to skirt them entirely. If they continued to move in the same direction down the fence line, I could pop out ahead of them and sneak in for a shot as the buck appeared to be leading the far-left edge of the group. It took an hour and a half of slipping in and out of the sparse cedars which dotted the terrain. At one point, I spooked a covey of grouse who ran mere feet from me, taunting me to loose a shaft at them as if they knew they were not the target that day.

I knew the area would begin to close in at the end of the field I was following the deer to, so I began to force my way into the problem I knew was coming ahead of me. The issue was the large swaths of old cattle fencing, namely buckthorn, waiting for me at the chokepoint, so I opted to fight it as much as possible. Navigating it was painfully slow, inching my way to the edge of an old, dried pond and watching as they began to bed down one by one. It now became a game of wait and see. At one point, a sudden gust of wind at my back blew my scent to where the deer had been only minutes earlier.

After several minutes, the buck stood up, walked to a small red pine, and began to rub his antlers, the brow tines shaving slim strips off the tree. He shook his head, sending the lower branches of the young conifer in all directions. Partially concealed, half sitting, half kneeling, I sat with my bow arm canted at a 45-degree angle to clear the brush. I hesitated to count his antler tines, not wanting to become fixated on his six-pointed crown. Their bases and mass were a dark chocolate color, due in part to the dense pine trees he had no doubt spent most of his fall rubbing, the pine tar binding with his brow tines. As he turned to look back at the does, I tried to get a shot off by covering several feet in a crouch and gaining some ground in his direction. Moving slowly and ensuring I had good stability, I raised the short recurve, launching the arrow across the meadow to where he stood, preoccupied with picking a windfall apple off the broken ground.

As I released the shaft, one of the does caught the motion and jumped several feet, but it was too late. I looked to see the buck faltering as he came to a halt next to a break in the fence line. The does were gone, running into the thick cover and darkness of the cedars, snorting and wheezing as they vacated the area. Several minutes later, I realized I had just taken my first spot and stalk whitetail as I walked up to him and sat down to take a breath. Running my hands across his neck and onto his antlers covered in pine tar, a sense of deep appreciation flooded over the moment as I paused to reflect on the life he led.

The wind began to pick up, whipping at the nearby trees as they bent to its will. The skies darkened with the promise of incoming snow. It was a long drag out to the canoe. With the sun dipping into the horizon, I began working on the deer and the task ahead. I had hunted that same area many times before and had been stymied by the wind or the deer's eyes as I snuck around in an attempt to accomplish what had just transpired.

I had failed in each one of those prior attempts. The difference was in having a solid strategy and tactics to work that piece of land, and the knowledge learned from the failure of those prior stalks. The learning process of the strategy hit home. Not everything had gone right that day. The wind had changed somewhat, and I was quickly running out of cover. The tactics had won the day. The prior failure of rushing too fast, not checking the wind, and not being patient enough had educated me and taught me to slow down and focus. Ethics and the inclusion of patience and confidence in my kit had spurred me on. The challenges presented on that day were a path I had walked many times prior and had failed in as many times.

If continuous success in bringing home game is the driver for you in traditional bowhunting, I will tell you that you will need to rethink that attitude. That's not to say you won't be successful, but this method of hunting is significantly more difficult simply because you need to get close and get good at it. That takes time and some luck. Embracing that difficulty is part of the learning curve.

I see examples of folks all the time adding to their bows setup or drastically modifying how they shoot or buying new camo clothes thinking that it will bring them increased success when all they need to do is get out in the woods and fields and hunt, full stop, end of story.

Don't get me wrong, it's your process, but I highly recommend keeping things simple for the new folks getting into this sport. Once you've got a good idea of what you're doing shot-wise, add or subtract from your equation and process.

A common problem I see all the time is folks getting into shooting a stickbow and going down the bunny hole of paralysis by analysis before they get a baseline for themselves, a yardstick of some flight time by which to measure their ability. It takes time, and I still shoot all year round to stay on point with my shooting. I do not deviate from what I know will work for me, in other words, the basics.

Know the area you're going to hunt and have terrain knowledge. Understand the habits of the animal you are hunting, its bedding areas, feeding areas, and movement routes according to the land and the season. Do your research and planning.

Know your limitations in both shooting and positions, ensuring you are fully confident in your equipment, and shoot in the clothing you will be wearing when hunting. Challenge yourself from adverse positions and ranges and add actual hunting shots into your practice so you can adapt and recognize good shot angles. I will only practice on quartering or broadside targets, so it is burned into my muscle memory to take high-percentage shots and recognize them cognitively when they present themselves.

That is the path of the traditional bow hunter. The process of true hunting. The path to woodsmanship, scouting and tracking that accompanies the code of traditional archery and walking the path of the ethical predator. For others, it is a way of communing, centering, and connecting with our past. In any regard and for whatever reason, this becomes an individual path. The lessons learned all those years ago from that first deer have shaped into a memory of work and effort, which still resonates with me today.

Chapter Six

The Inevitable

Reconcile the Inner Hunter

L ike many folks, I am drawn as much to the wild as I am inexorably to hunting the hard way. The inevitable connection it brings as we are drawn one step closer to a simpler time in our chaotic human pattern is, I believe, one of the primary drivers for this.

Hunting with a stick and string does that; it pushes us ethically to hunt close. At the same time, it lets the ego check us and frees us of the restraints of everyday society if we are allowed to slip off the collar and run free, so to speak, to be one with the woods and fields. I have found that nothing brings me to the present as much as hunting traditionally does. I have always been more at home in the trees, swamps, and rivers of my life than ever in the concrete and paved cities we have erected. It connects me to my ancestry and the "wild" part of who I truly am.

After spending long durations in the woods, cold, tired, hungry, and often with no modern conveniences, a heated modern home is appreciated on a much different level. I firmly believe people would genuinely appreciate what they have, not what they lack, quite a bit more if they spent some time in the forests. Venturing out and experiencing some discomfort for even a limited time would give them some perspective that many these days could use.

There is a part of hunting, a piece of the path and process, that little is spoken of. It is synonymous with hunting of all types, yet it is, for me, the critical part of hunting with a stick-bow that directly forces being ethical and discerning in my hunting shots on game.

Anyone young or old has felt what I am speaking of; a subject that deserves more light than the darkness it typically gets: the unrecovered game animal.

Almost all hunting shows and videos primarily only show success. Less so the ability in the hard part of the process that may not seem as heroic or glamorous to the viewer. It does not matter if that loss is from a poor hit, poor shooting or poor tracking ability, or any of the other anomalies that can and do happen when hunting. If you hunt, it will happen. You will lose game. You will wound animals, and it will affect you in one way or another. It is the truth, and coming to terms with this and, more importantly, how to mitigate it is essential.

Many moons ago, I taught the archery and bowhunting portion of the hunter safety course here in the province. During that time, during the in-class parts and range demos, I emphasized that the bow was a close-range weapon. It always fascinated people to learn about archery hunting and the process it took to be proficient with a bow. However, as I have said prior, these days we are moving farther away in the shot and distance game with bowhunting in general and technology specifically. And in doing so, moving farther away from ethics. Coming to terms with all of this is not easy for some, and for good reason. Bowhunting can be for everyone, but it's also not for everyone.

I feel unparalleled appreciation when I am successful in the arrowing of game. Still, I have also felt the gut-wrenching sickness when the realization hits that I am unlikely to recover the animal I just shot. Indeed, those early-year hunting safety courses I assisted in were the best platform to make people aware of the importance of ethical shot distance and placement. Nowadays, everywhere you turn, there's a new hunting show featuring 70, 80, and 100-yard shots on game, with frontal shots all vetted and justified because someone else did it. If they did it on the 3D range, then that must make it doable in real life. Sadly, it's what we are not seeing as much as what we are not talking about in the loss of the game we pursue. Those hero shows do not show the misses, the wounding, or the poorer shots taken, all in the name of entertainment. I get it; they need to sell to make money. Tech sells, new products sell, and frankly, I have said it before; I don't give a good damn about what someone hunts with as long as they stay within the boundaries of their equipment, abilities, and remain ethical.

I was having a conversation some time ago with a member of a big game committee regarding the abundant use of crossbows in our province as opposed to actual archery hunting. He looked me squarely in the face and said, "Of course it's easier with a crossbow, but success sells! We have more hunters in the woods than ever with crossbows in the extended archery season." "We sure do," I retorted, "and you seem to have forgotten the entire reason why the season was so long in the first place; limitations of the equipment and difficulty impeded success rates." The conversation turned into a polite argument about anti-hunting and the big tent idea of hunting. Still, in some cases, the generous seasons and high success rates bring attention and the heat and light of reduced seasons. The starter package for most new crossbow hunters includes massive bait piles and a scoped weapon that can be shot accurately right out of the box with little skill or preparation.

These days the switch needs to be thrown back to what the original archery/primitive weapon seasons were meant for: hunting with a weapon that required skill, time, patience, and the necessity to get close. The game departments understood that it was to be more challenging, and in that difficulty was born an appreciation for being a good archer and hunter. Thus, a bowhunter, the synthesis of the two, was born.

I always tell the people I coach that stickbow hunting is 50 percent effective shooting and 50 percent effective hunting skills with luck sprinkled on top of the whole process. This chapter is about difficulty, hard work, and, unfortunately, the loss accompanying being a hunter.

I had gotten up late (working the night before until 1:00 a.m. hadn't helped). I rushed to get out the door, into the truck, and to the back of my folks' property where I was deer hunting the archery only season. It was almost a half hour after sunrise, and I was worried; it was nearly the end of the pre-rut, and I knew the deer would be moving.

I had passed up shots at two different bucks and a large doe two days prior as they ran by me at full pelt. The chase was full on. I sat on the west side of a dense cedar swamp and blowdown that was a regular travel corridor and convergence trail between a large bedding and feeding area. Deciding not to take the usual route into my stand, I was concerned that I would be walking right into the feeding area and spooking any deer already moving through the transition area.

I walked the shorter route around the edge of an old sandpit area that had once held lumber from an old skid system back when the access roads were built 100 years prior. A grouse strutted along the edge just feet away from me, a large adult male with a solid tail fan and large black ruffs. I paused with my half-raised bow, but my mind wasn't on grouse that morning.

My eyes fixated on a pine tree that had been rubbed clear of all the bark on one side for almost two feet. The rub was extremely fresh, maybe only a few hours old, and pine tar was running slowly out of several large gouges due to the buck's brow tines raking the young tree far past its armor of bark. I stopped and knelt, looking down at the large hoof prints in the mud and the kicked-up moss where the buck had turned and continued to the lip of the berm where I intended to cross.

A light wind was in my favor, blowing across the old pond, now more like an overgrown meadow with only a small bit of water at the south end. I paused as I did every time I walked by that pond as if I was waiting for a pair of teal or wood ducks to take flight into the air like on every duck stamp of my childhood. The buck's tracks were deep and stood out from the others on the worn game trail parallel to my line of travel. The grouse had enough and rocketed out of the scrub, flying into a nearby birch tree, staring arrogantly at me with its crest up, like royalty being disturbed by my presence in his royal garden. The bird's sudden explosion from the leaves woke me from my trance, staring at the large deer tracks. I looked back at the pine tree, nervous and concerned that I had fouled things up by waking up late and fumbling my way into the stand.

The woods were quiet; it had rained the night before, so the crisp, fallen leaves felt like a wet carpet that morning.

My mind went back to when I had picked this oak, which to others, may have been too low to the ground for a stand. I was up maybe 11 feet off the ground. This tree stand covered a broad convergence of three trails and was close to bedding and feeding areas so that deer could move back and forth between them. The best part was that it was in a transition area where coniferous and deciduous trees came together, forming a sparse gap 75 yards long with a secondary trail that ran within 15 feet of the stand, providing excellent gaps for shooting.

The wind typically prevailed southeast, which was beneficial since even with evening thermal winds, it blew my scent away from the bedding areas and across the trail into the roadway where I had parked one and a half miles away.

I had little to clear for shooting lanes as I guessed the trail to be only 20 feet away from the tree and well within my effective range with my recurve. It gave me time to hear and see deer coming down any of the three trails: two from the bedding areas and one from the feeding area by the old oak. In the past, I stood on the stand and shot arrows at stumps and leaves that littered the trail. At the same time, my Springer spaniel ran around chasing rabbits and juvenile wood ducks off the nearby pond, having to recall the stout rough-coat dog back several times as she drove game from the area with gusto. However, on this day, the rabbits and fowl were free to go about their business, as she was at home waiting for me to return to show her displeasure at not tagging along.

I made my way to the oak, walking through a mess of small pines, their limbs slapping my face as I wove in and around them. Avoiding the main run, I tried to peer at the trail to see if the same tracks from the rubbed pine had gone down the path past my stand. After hooking my bow to the pull rope and donning the safety belt, I climbed up like a giant insect to the stand without a hitch. I hauled the recurve up, nocked an arrow, then looked around at the main trail that ran across the front of the stand.

A crosswind wind picked up, which concerned me. Either way, I thought, I am out here, so I may as well make the best of it. I sat for the entire day and had only brought a granola bar. The movements I made digging the bar out of my pocket raised the ire of the red squirrels my youngest calls "fur rattlers" due to their chiding barks.

I was sitting on a small portable stand a buddy had given me. It was not a large platform but was easy to toss into a tree in a hurry and weighed very little. I settled in after checking my safety belt.

It always seems to be something of a miracle when a deer appears when one is hunting big woods or swamp whitetails; one moment, they are not there, then suddenly appearing out of nowhere. That's precisely what happened; I had been watching the skies grow grey as the sun hung below the clouds framed against pines to my east when a buck appeared from a thicket. I had not expected a deer to come from there. He did not use either trail I expected but was making his way directly to me. A respectable large-bodied six-point, he appeared 70 yards in front of me, walking in on the main trail. I love seeing big antlered bucks, but I love eating venison far more than big antlers, and as my grandfather would say, "You can't roast antlers." This deer would do nicely. Besides, if I'd waited for the biggest racked deer to walk by over my hunting career, I likely would have rarely tasted venison. Our whitetail population is around six to 10 deer per square mile and does have higher densities in some areas over others; still, our herd in Ontario is roughly under half of what Michigan has in population numbers.

The buck ambled closer checking his back trail frequently; the wind was good, blowing steadily out of the north. It was now or never, I thought and stood very slowly. I focused on the crease of his shoulder three-quarters of the way down from his spine, intently watching as he came closer. I managed to slowly shift into a good position, bringing the bow up and bending at my waist, leaned out, and waited for several minutes until the deer turned to his right to present the quartering-away shot I wanted. I shot when he was 20 yards out - well within my effective lethal range. The arrow flew well, then appeared to kick a little high as if it deflected. The arrow hit the buck, and he scrambled away, not stopping for anything.

I sat down, took a few deep breaths, and focused on a tree where the buck had disappeared. The shot had looked good. "No problem," I thought. "I'll get down in 30 minutes and look." As sure as I was about where that arrow had gone, I didn't like the way the arrow had kicked. I tried to ignore that and stood up, looking for the arrow. As I began to climb down, the wind picked up from the direction the deer had vaulted. With my feet back on terra firma, I examined the arrow's flight path.

I could see it plainly from the ground now. It had been almost invisible from my perch, but it was there as if it had grown in front of me while I sat in the tree: a small, contorted swamp maple about a meter high. The top branch, around a quarter of an inch thick, was cut and hanging, sliced by the broadhead enroute to the whitetail. The arrow was nowhere to be seen.

I stopped and marked the little tree, no more than a sprig coming out of the ground, then cursed myself for not clearing it from that direction. "Too late now." I thought.

I unhooked my haul rope and realized I had left my larger pack in the truck when I walked in, stuffing my license, tag, and wallet into my smaller fanny pack. Taking care not to make too much noise, I walked back to my truck. I want to say that

I recovered that animal, but sadly I did not. The area where I was hunting is part of a more extensive swamp system known simply as the "Long Swamp." Several factors played a role in creating the perfect storm for non-recovery.

It was at one time part of a larger river system long before settlers had trod on this part of the earth. It was still massive, although reduced to a long, winding, extended swamp of blowdowns and beaver dams with a small creek running through. Movement in its inner cordons was treacherous and full of deadheads and partially dried-up beaver ponds full of four-foot-deep muck. I had hunted its fringes for years with some success, as the deer loved the cover and food it provided, but the inner breaks where I hunted on that day challenged the hunter in me.

Returning with my tracking pack and flashlight, I searched for the arrow. After almost 20 minutes of finding nothing but some grey hair at the shot site, I opted to head to the last location I had seen him.

The last I had seen the buck, he was running by an old weathered birch. It had begun to perish some years earlier but was still hanging on to life in its upper branches. Its upper trunk was hollowed by weather and insects, providing a nesting spot for a merlin over the past decade, but now abandoned until the following spring sun. My father had sat in the tree years earlier before the onset of its demise, and I recalled meeting him one evening when I was much younger after he had arrowed a large doe with his American semi-longbow, a time when the area was still open and navigable. The area had significantly changed since an ice storm ravaged the area years prior. Standing under the tree, I saw the shaft just beyond its falling bark. The arrow was lying on the ground, its autumn orange shaft stark against the olive greens and browns of the swamp floor. Studying the blood and hair on the shaft, I saw the hair was a lighter brown than I would have liked to see. I had hit the deer, but the blood was darker than I wanted and there was no sign of oxygenated blood. I tracked for maybe 100 yards, and although I had some blood, the distance between the sign was almost 10 yards and spotty. I knew from the sign and tracks that the buck had been running all out and directly into the tall grasses and buckthorn-choked tangles in the middle of the old swamp.

Two hours had passed since the shot, and I was about to call it quits and back out. I had been on my hands and knees due to the thick brush when a croaking sound caught my ears.

The wind picked up as I looked skyward at two ravens, looking like flying black triangles against the dark grey backdrop of nimbus formations as if beckoning me to retire. Flying prognosticators of what was about to befall me. As their croaking grew distant, drops of rain touched my bow hand as I looked high into the sky and prayed it wouldn't rain any heavier.

There was no rain forecast for today, I thought. No, not until tomorrow, which is why I had gone out that afternoon and not the following day. By that time, I surmised, the deer was long expired if the arrow had gone where I thought it had. Darkness was falling. I spent another hour looking for sign after it began to rain. I was frustrated and concerned; that gut-wrenching feeling began in my stomach.

Stopping, I turned off the flashlight and knelt next to a large stump, collecting my thoughts. What to do? I had no assistance, and it was dark and raining steadily now. Pack up, and come back in the morning, I rationalized. I opted to back out, lest I ruin any sign and possibly stumble by the deer in the dark and not see it. That's when I heard them off to my right, maybe less than 100 yards northwest, as I exited the last thicket before hitting the old tote trail to my truck.

Their mournful yelps and yipping soon turned to howls and barking, the cedar canopy above me swaying back and forth to their cries. I knew a pack of coyotes, the locals called "brush wolves," had been south of me a couple of kilometers away that year. I had heard them yelling at the train as it passed off the highway at dark several times already that fall. All genetic dispositions aside, those dogs were far better than I at tracking, and my concern grew. I didn't sleep much that night.

I was back out at first light. The sun's rising created shadows of greens and browns washing over the area that was now dripping wet from the downpour only hours ago. I searched again and found no blood; all evidence had washed away. However, I had a direction of travel and opted to locate his tracks and find him that way. The meat should be fine, as it was cold the night before. I tried to remain optimistic. Crawling and creeping, I pushed through a tangle of buckthorn and blowdowns, trying a grid method of search, but still nothing. It was not to be.

I spent that day and the next morning looking to no avail. Disheartened, I walked back to my truck to contemplate the events; the season was not over, but I wouldn't feel like hunting for the next week.

Later that afternoon, a landowner out mowing found him; he had made it almost 250 yards from where I had made the shot before expiring and being picked clean by the coyotes.

I gave the antlers to the farmer and called the provincial Conservation Officer in our area to let him know what had happened. He was surprised that I'd looked for him for two and a half days. Then, before packing it in, I attempted to re-trace the track the buck had taken from where I'd found the arrow. He died almost 100 yards from where I had lost the blood trail. It appeared he had turned, still running flat out at that point with the coyotes hot on his heels. He had not bedded down once from any sign I found, and except for a smear of blood on a tree, I found no other trace. I estimated he had turned when the coyotes suddenly got on him and did his death run into the open area onto the neighboring property. It would not have taken him long to cover that distance at a dead run.

I had lost the buck to a combination of factors, some under my control and others not:

1. The deflected shot. I had not seen the small yearling tree three yards in front of the animal. It was enough to deflect the arrow farther back and higher than I had intended.

2. I may have seen him drop if it had been across open cover or a field, and tracking would have been much easier.

3. No matter what the forecast says, measure your hunting by this with your terrain and know the area as best you can.

Knowledge of the terrain is critical to being a good tracker. Had I known it would rain heavily that night, I may not have hunted that area and opted instead for a more open stand setup or waited for the rain to let up and hunted later that week. Weather and terrain should always be a focus of the pre-hunt strategy. Use mapping and weather apps, check for temperature and pressure drops that can trigger precipitation, and ensure you're ready to track with the necessary tools. The importance of that experience should not be lost on and discarded by any hunter. If anything, the learning curve should jump, and an effort made to assess what happened, what was in the realm of control, and what was not. That was the first, but not the last, animal I would lose. I've lost a couple of others, as will anyone who has hunted for any length of time with any weapon.

I hunted the remainder of that season and passed on two other bucks a little out of my comfort zone as they quickly walked over 35 yards away. I wasn't about to poke out that far at that point. I hunt that swamp to this day, but I am picky about when I do, often preferring to wait until the snow flies. I have taken several deer from its jungle in the past several years.

It is easier to hunt in that mess and pattern the deer with snow on the ground. I have also learned to set up on the breaks and edges.

I have found that unrecovered animals is a topic that most hunters, regardless of the weapon, do not speak of much or tell many folks, if anyone. The problem is that all hunters, humans, raptors, canids, bears, and even big cats like cougars and lions wound and lose prey that eventually expires. We are apex predators, and we can learn much to assess our abilities as hunters best by keeping our egos in check and staying within the reasonable limits of the fish and wildlife laws and our equipment's capabilities.

Someone recently verbally bombed me for critiquing a person's black bear hunt on social media. I commented on the chosen shot placement with his compound on a black bear - a facing frontal shot - maybe slight quartering to the right. Did the bear expire? Yes. Did the fellow make a once-in-a-lifetime shot? Yes! One hundred percent he did! But due to the shot placement, he did not get a pass-through and had it been a poor hit, there would have been an insufficient blood trail. He also served to poorly educate other folks by encouraging the same, exhibiting poor ethical considerations.

Ethics in hunting is not just about you; it's about the animal as well. These days, when questioned about why they did not wait for a better angle before taking the shot, the reaction is as if all of "hunting" itself is getting attacked. Nothing could be farther from the truth. About that particular bear, anyone who understands bear anatomy knows damn well how much bone, cartilage, and muscle you need to get through within the small window that hunter had to thread to get an arrow into that bear. Now, hear me out, and I speak from experience here, having tracked and recovered and lost a few animals of my own. I have also tracked and recovered other hunters animals for almost 40 years. I have taught quite a few folks what I was taught as a youth and what I have learned along the way. My intent here is not to lecture, far from it, but to stop and think for a minute about the whole process of what we are doing.

My base intent is to provide food for my family that is free range and free of antibiotics and other chemicals used in large-scale animal production. The animals I hunt have valid lives; they are not caged or fed hormones to grow faster and fatter. No, they are wild, and for as long as humanoids have been walking the earth, they have been hunted. We co-exist and have a relationship that stretches back long before big box stores and lineups at the supermarket. That relationship has faded and, in doing so, has made us weaker as a species with a reliance on the grocery store for food. I firmly believe that making that connection brings us much closer to who we really are as humans and increases our need to protect the wild places we still have left and the animals and fauna that live there. That relationship through bowhunting depends solely on me and my decision to release the arrow as efficiently as possible within my effective lethal range! Ok, so you've heard me go off about that term in the past, but what does it mean?

Despite the obvious connotations, it has to do with both the mentality and intent in finding the spatial relationship between you and the animal you intend to shoot where you are absolutely, without a doubt effective at placing that arrow where it needs to go. There is no hesitation, no doubt, no struggle stick, nothing but lethal intent.

You've trained, practiced, individualized, functionalized, and maintained your shooting ability with whatever weapons platform you choose. Only you know what that range is and where to put that arrow into an animal and ensure to the best of your ability that it goes there.

That mentality has zero struggle stick thoughts; missing does not come into play, neither does any apprehension of the weapon, in my case a stickbow - a recurve to be exact - and its ability to send a broadhead tipped shaft to its target with lethal results. Because what's on the end of the arrow is what does the job, an arrow does not kill by hydro-static shock like a bullet. It needs to cut, penetrate and sever arteries and vitals. Your focus should always be that of a hunter who wants to ensure the game you pull the string on goes down as quickly and lethally as possible. That mental game must be as sharp as the broadhead on your shaft! Anything less in your intention will not cut it (pardon the pun).

Now stop for a minute; let's talk about that because we all don't want the game we pursue to suffer, but as good hunters, we must come to terms with the fact that we may lose game. Anomalies and outliers in hunting happen; it is not absent from the process. It is the ultimate test of your mental ethics game and should be the primary driver for getting as good as you can and staying razor-sharp in shooting all year round, not just when the season is firing up. Good shooting ability with your equipment should be primary; the vehicle for that is to reduce the chance of wounding game. There should be no doubts, no hesitation, or excuses. If you are lazy, your shot will be lazy. If you're not confident, it will show. If you are tired, it will show in your shooting. If you're aware and awake, your shooting will be as well. Pressure, flight time, and consistency are necessary. None of these principles are about ego or machismo. Far from that, it comes from a part embedded in us as humans and is connected to empathy and the ability to control our decisions.

We intend to be efficient, make that decision to be nothing less than the effective hunters we are and can be, with prudence and focused intent, to reduce the factors that prevent you from recovering an animal. We will cover a few of the factors that I have come across.

Distance is the one factor we can control. I have seen folks say they were X distance from the animal, and their stated distance was way off. When the adrenaline starts pumping, our brain goes on autopilot. Reacting to that high-stress stimulus, we all go through an Observe, Orient, Decision, Act (OODA) loop. Unless we train ourselves to go through an OODA loop and relate our archery shooting to it, we will not control ourselves as efficiently. In other words, slowing down that process and taking control through various stressors and pressure shooting will help, but experience will help most of all. It's simple. The farther away from an animal you are, the higher the risk of something bad happening; the animal changes direction, moves even slightly, or another animal gets in the way. Suffice it to say, and I've said it before, the farther away you move in shot presentation, the farther you move away from good ethics. And just because the hero of the hunting show did it does not mean everyone can. It's TV, and it needs to sell. I cringe when I see this happening. Youth see it, and it plants the seed they can make that shot, too, which is not a realistic goal.

In essence, bows are not high-velocity weapons; they are not rifles and bragging about that elk you took at 80 yards is talking about a risky shot, not a sure thing. Anything less, and you're doing the art of bowhunting and, more importantly, the animal a disservice and displaying a total lack of respect. In any case, you're leaving your shot open to anomalies outside the realm of consistency on live animals. 3-D is one thing, but again foam doesn't move.

Penetration is critical, and all bow hunters should be looking for a shot that gets double penetration, a pass-through, in one side and out the other for a better blood trail. That is one of the main reasons I am dead against frontal or front-quartering shots. I have seen more animals lost to this shot than any other. Yes, some expired quickly, and some did not, but the lost animals had no exit wound resulting in a very poor to no blood trail. Tree stand shots usually produce better blood trails because you have a downward exit wound.

Be a good bow hunter, not just a good shooter. Yes, there is a difference. Get close and get used to being close.

Anatomical research: do your homework on the species you're hunting. Bone is a problem no matter how heavy or front-of-center your arrow is. Take the time to look at vitals charts and watch real live deer. Get used to their movements when relaxed, spooky, and alert.

Now, on to broadheads. I have seen many animals taken with different broadheads and hits. I am not going to debate about mechanical heads, but generally, I have seen poor penetration and blade failure from hitting bone. That is something that can and will happen. Cut-on-contact heads are the way to go, and for what I teach, the only way. Go with an excellent cut-on-contact head that you can sharpen well and flies well off your setup. I highly recommend a three-blade head for new folks as they have a tri-cutting surface that leaves good entry and exit wounds. And, in my opinion, they are easier to sharpen. Since arrow flight equals good placement and penetration, ensure that you're getting that off your setup with broadheads, not just the same weight field points.

Animal behavior and clearance are factors, of course, and any bowhunter who has had a branch or tree jump into the path of their arrow knows this. If I am setting up, I am extremely careful to ensure clearly defined shooting lanes, taking arrow trajectory into account. Stay within the laws set forth by your province or state; this may seem obvious, and I am not arguing the efficiency of anyone's equipment by any means but diverting from those laws paints all bow hunters in a bad light. A well placed sharp broadhead from a decent hunting weight bow will efficiently take most, if not all, big game ethically.

The issue lies with those pesky anomalies; animal movement, bone, and, again, the ability to penetrate and ensure the animal expires quickly. Mitigate those anomalies with patience and good control, and take only shots you are 100 percent confident in.

No two tracking jobs are ever the same. Get used to tracking; go slow. When you're on the trail and have doubts, back off, get out, and get help. Tracking in the sunlight is also much easier than in the dark, regardless of the best of flashlights. I also encourage folks for those anomaly tracking problems to find someone with a tracking dog ahead of hunting season if allowed in your area. In Ontario, we are allowed a dog to track wounded game if it is under control and meets a minimum leash requirement. I have trained two of our Weimaraner's to track deer, and on three occasions, due to weather, we have recovered animals that could have been lost. Check your local game laws for more info.

And finally, when it comes to your shooting, use a consistent method where you are burning those patterns into your neurological pathways. Doing so allows you to be ready when the adrenaline hits and you're prepping your shot. The question is about pressure and how you will handle it with your training in shooting and experience.

When you're exposed to elements, no shot is a "cold shot." Your blood pressure and heart rate will go up, your adrenal glands will kick in, and you will be warmed up. Take your time, don't rip the string back, know your limits and hey, guess what? Maybe it doesn't work out, and you don't get that shot? Then better luck next time.

Subjectively assessing what occurred is not dwelling on the loss but learning from it. It gives honor to the process and the animal's life. It will also help to prevent it from happening again and make you a much more effective and ethical hunter. That's why it's called hunting and not shooting.

Chapter Seven

Archers Paradox & Pheasants

Instinctive Draw

My effort in shooting had ultimately become a method of training as I began to see comparisons in shooting my bow instinctively and close-quarter combat shooting applications: Look at the target, whatever that target is, post on it, and shoot for center mass; but I'm getting ahead of myself. How the heck can that apply to shooting a bow instinctively? Part of the problem lies in some folk's definition of what instinctive shooting is; some perceive it as some ethereal magical process of manifesting that arrow to the target, but it is not. If anything, shooting instinctively could be called "intuitive shooting" and is quite the opposite of anything magical. Frankly, it takes time, effort, and development to become proficient, just like anything else.

As I have stated previously, it's much like the attributes of casting a fly rod to a rising fish, tossing a football to a receiver under pressure, or shouldering & pointing a shotgun at a fast-flying bird. Each has a process and training method for building a skill set surrounding hand-eye coordination and focus—all crucial components for success. Getting back to my original statement, in addition to these components, it is critical to note that these comparisons and evolutions have been formed from actual applied hunting conditions under pressure, not sanitized comfortable target shooting, or the same repetitive structures under the same conditions. Enter the *"live-string."*

It was past noon, and the sun had emerged from behind a bank of clouds that had left a flour dusting of snow on the late autumn ground. I had been walking down the dirt road, accompanied by our Weimaraner, for nearly 20 minutes. I had tagged out on deer already and was anticipating a pleasant stroll with the dog. Coming around a bend, the dog stopped and locked up on point only to flashpoint again, run forward, and lock up like a piece of furry granite on something beyond the cedar fence bordering the road. I stepped forward, and a coyote leaped from its hiding place and bolted across the opposite field, kicking up a cloud of snow in its wake. The dog turned back and looked at me, unimpressed. I, too, was not pleased as the ground entering that field was littered with the footprints of pheasants we were after that day.

Concerned the wild dog had been through the area we were walking to, I strained to see through the glaring sun for the opening to the field the landowner had directed us to enter his property. It was much farther than the farmer had implied, but we found it, nonetheless.

Shouldering the recurve, I unhitched the gate latch and let the dog into the extensive acreage. The gate creaked back into place like some ancient drawbridge, and I latched it tight again as per the landowner's instructions. The area was open with several piles of brush and three ditches for irrigation running across it. A large patch of cattails lined the back end where a stream and swamp lay adjacent to the cornfield. There were signs of birds; dozens of tracks littered the ground, many more than I had expected; almost all of them headed into the half-cut corn stalks left standing at the end of the first field. Usually, I would have had my over and under with a load of #6 in the barrels and with me, but the township had a "no firearms discharge" order close to the town limits, so the only weapon allowed was the bow.

This area was part of an old overgrown farm used only in the front end for corn harvest. It was a long walk but well worth it in the end. It is one of the only areas in the province accessible for me to hunt wild birds. They thrived on the large property due to the good amount of available cover and lake effects, allowing for a reduced snowpack during the winter.

I had wanted to ask the owner for almost three years. I knew him through a mutual friend from trout fishing the stream's upper reaches, where it exited a golf course several miles beyond. I understood wild pheasants ran rampant through the old agricultural area.

One morning a year prior in April, while I was plying a nymph for trout in the stream's upper reaches, I heard birds crowing back and forth, and it stirred the youth in me to return in the fall. Here remnant princes existed, wild, cagey, and resilient birds left over from the early 1900's stockings in the province. As a kid, pheasant had always been a mystical creature. My grandfather had spoken of them in reverence, and the few I did happen to run into always held my gaze with a sense of old-school nostalgia, envisioning a rising pheasant and a barn in the backdrop in my mind.

I had hunted birds on the wing with a bow before, as well as ducks and geese in my youth. I had also lost plenty of arrows in those attempts and had successfully taken a couple of mallards and Canada geese by decoying to flock setups in large fields. I had several flu-flus in my quiver, all tipped with older broadheads too worn for deer but necessary to bring a down pheasant. Flying shots would be the only safe choice since, with the pup along, I could not risk attempting ground shots.

The snow made no noise as I watched the dog's tail wagging with short brisk twitches of excitement as she worked the first drainage ditch. We walked up, skimming in a zig-zag pattern as she tried to catch the scent of the birds. Soon, the dog locked up, and I hastily nocked an arrow. "Whoa, girl," I advised as she pointed toward a small blowdown with several waste grain stalks bent over like tents in a perfect row. I slowly stepped forward, trying to figure out where the bird may be and what trajectory it would take. Nothing. Another step, this time right into the cornstalks. Nothing moved, I turned to my dog, and she had that adamant "It is in there" look on her grey muzzle. Turning back, I began to circle slowly, faced the sun, and stomped the ground as I trudged into the small thicket. A large jackrabbit burst from the patch and ran with lightning speed across the berms into the cut corn and another thicket some distance away, enticing me to shoot, but the sounds of a nervous rooster were coming from the tangles. For the pup's sake, I refrained from sending a pointy stick his way lest the dog break point.

"A rabbit?" I asked the dog, now looking at her directly. She moved forward quickly, head low, like a silver panther, and locked up again on point. I turned, almost out of sheer knowledge of what was beyond my control now, and the large rooster rocketed up directly behind me, only feet away into the sky like a feathered fireball shooting for the sun. Tugging the string back on the stout recurve, I let the arrow fly after the sky-high bird a mere 15 feet away and watched it sail harmlessly over its back while the escaping bird cackled at my misfortune. The dog bolted forward several feet until she stopped to watch the pheasant land and run for the cover of the cattails like a soldier running for a trench line across no man's land. She looked at me disapprovingly, as only a bird dog can. Anyone who has hunted behind a bird dog will know exactly what that look is and how easily they can communicate it. That was not my first time trying to arrow a pheasant; only prior they had been incidental as I had ground sluiced a couple I had come across in my youth while hunting for cottontails on my grandparents' place.

As a kid, I watched American Sportsman with my grandfather. I was awestruck by Fred Bear, arguably one of the Fathers and true icons of traditional archery, snatching pheasants from the air with his recurve. In a way, I was living a childhood dream, but this was on another level. Wild birds and cold weather were a far cry from a cozy living room and my late grandfather's armchair. I'd practiced aerial shooting for a couple of weeks when I had time and had even broken several hand-thrown clay birds tossed up for me.

I stopped to assess the situation, concerned that this was the only bird we would get onto that day and thinking about how to cover the remainder of the field tactfully. I recovered the arrow, a red-barred turkey fletched flu-flu tipped with a well-worn Zwickey Delta broadhead.

Touching up the worn edges on the head, I knelt to pet the dog, thanked her for her efforts, and gave her a drink. She sniffed the arrow fletch and the recurve, then looked at me again, almost as if to say, "Dude, where's the shotgun?!"

We picked up where we left off, working across the opposite drainage ditch. That resulted in a couple more points, one hen that sat and looked at us before walking off indignantly, seemingly fully aware that she was off limits for us, and a wild flush of two roosters that kept running on the dog as she tried to pin them down to no avail. Watching them fly across the field to safety, I turned to face the sun and saw the dog suddenly lock up on a small cluster of grapevines adjoining a brush pile of buckthorn. Walking and checking my string, I stepped around a large branch that had fallen over the running water nearby. I was distracted by two brook trout as I stepped over the small stream to reach the dogs point, their haloed back vermiculation's being admired by both the sun shining in the tea-colored holding water and myself as the ancient char tails fanned slowly in the edge of the riffle, several feet from my path. Turning back to the dog, who had now locked up tight again, I released my mind from the trout and pushed it back to the business of the ringnecks.

Bending around the brush pile the dog was staring intently at, her short tail quivering, "bird," I tightened my grip on the bowstring as the rooster launched straight up 15 feet or so and then arced slightly to the right as the bow came up. I swung through the bird and loosed the arrow. I clearly recall coming to full draw, seeing only the bird and, in slow motion, the arrow catching it at the wing pinion and neck in a cloudburst of golden and painted feathers.

After the arrow passed through and out of the bird, he fell, tumbling to the ground. I stood motionless, looking at the arrow 50 yards beyond the bird's final flight and sticking into the ground like a red flag of victory. I hollered "back" to the dog, and she retrieved the bird, wagging her feelings for me to see her happiness at doing precisely what she had been bred for. I hastily tucked the bird into my vest and stooped to water the dog.

The shot had happened all by itself, and the event's impact began to trickle down and strike me with the realization that I had just arrowed a flying pheasant at almost 20 yards. We rounded the field and managed to pin down two more birds, connecting cleanly with another.

That was a turning point in my instinctive shooting evolution and connection to a kinetic process of using a bow and arrow; within the development of the instinctive shooting method, I now help folks develop their own abilities. It was a snapshot, as some would say, after hitting my anchor pocket and coming to full draw, but the shot prep for the birds had really hit home with me.

I am not speaking of the aerial practice beforehand nor the angle of the approach I had used after the dog had gone on point; No, I am speaking to the connection with the bow and my draw hand. I realized that day that when I drew, I shot naturally with form, but I was deadly accurate without robotic preparation.

The point and draw process was critical, combined with focusing on the center mass of the bird. That hit home to me and resulted in a series of drills I developed to focus on arrow placement when shooting at game, not just picking a spot. I now understood I was already in the shot process as soon as I had my hand engaging the string with dynamic tension; this was where "live-string" was born. That kinaesthetic connection to my bow arm and draw hand synched together out of the pressure of the hunt, not the target range or even roving. That was a fundamental aspect that produced a natural result. This method allowed me to swing through the birds, like pointing and swinging a shotgun.

That land I hunted and the area it stood on is now a large housing development. The trout are gone from the stream, now used as sewer drainage. The pup is no longer as well, leaving memories of a cherished grey ghost with staunch points and an always happy tail.

However far behind in time those memories are, stands a day that still resonates with me soundly. I became a better archer that day, but more importantly, a much more effective bowhunter as I entered the live-string process.

Over the years, I have heard many definitions of "instinctive archery." Many people have also told me that it does not actually exist. Suffice it to say I tend to go by my own experiences, influences, and practical approaches. I do not, however, preach that my way is the only way and that all other ways are deficient. This attitude is, to some degree, infecting both traditional bowhunting and other forms of hunting these days, much the same way fly fishing became elitist in many ways years ago. Instinctive archery, particularly in the context of bowhunting, and what I am teaching at Primitive Stone Archery, is about developing a fundamental method of shooting a trad bow with good basic structure and consistency and, in doing so, teaching the individual how to shoot intuitively. I like to step back and watch when I train folks to shoot using the natural abilities of their kinaesthetic perception coupled with our principle of Look-Point-Shoot, one arrow at a time, and developing the individual's personal method of shooting a traditional bow that suits their unique attributes & weapon.

Enter the live-string draw process. Live-string tension is a crucial step and component of the Archers Trinity shooting method. Live-string initiates the entire draw cycle and engages the kinaesthetic perception of the draw process. It engages back tension naturally and mentally prepares you for the shot. Once you connect with your bow kinaesthetically, it will be easier to focus on your sight picture, whatever that may be, and shoot your bow the way that works best for you.

This basic principle will help you to develop your specific rhythm and structure in time, and with repetition and flow, you will build consistency with flight time.

Being able to shoot instinctively will become a natural process and eliminate the mystery some folks seem to perceive about instinctive shooting that you cannot find on google or YouTube videos.

My father's teachings years ago in consistent shooting under pressure allowed me to develop my process. Dabbling in field archery and 3D in my youth led me to research and, under pressure and flight time, create the Archers Trinity Instinctive Shooting method, ultimately born of learning how to hunt and become effective with a traditional bow.

My influence comes from none of the current shot experts and gurus, many of whom claim loudly that if you don't shoot their way, then you are taking chances. Nothing could be further from the truth. Shooting of any kind, specifically with a traditional bow, is a uniquely individual process. I have had several folks inspire me along the way, two being Paul Brunner and Fred Asbell. However, as a once wise and famous martial artist, the late Bruce Lee was fond of saying, "Add what is specifically your own."

As humans, we tend to overthink things that give us difficulty, and you've heard me talk of this process before, paralysis by analysis. Instinctive shooting takes time and training; there's no magic, just correct practice and time. It won't happen overnight, and if you're not having fun, well, there is something wrong. Be teachable and open yourself up to time and patience. We are all individuals, and a system of shooting that teaches a foundation for which the individual can grow from and into their way of shooting frees one from the dogma of elitism, which is causing all methods of hunting, not just with trad bows, to become an us against them mentality in which we as hunters all lose.

Chapter Eight

Instinctive Art Honed

Effort in Arrow Flight

Yes, it's an art. In its truest form, bowhunting is a kinetic human-trait art of casting projectiles, whether we care to come to terms with the fact we are all born from hunter-gatherers or not. Hunting the hard way was normal for bowhunters in the not-so-distant past, and if you think on it enough, you will ponder what drives us to head into the woods with various bows and sharpened sticks to try to get close enough to wild game with our strung instruments.

When everything seems to fall into place effortlessly, when we become so involved in our connection to the wild places, we pursue game in that it just seems so natural. There are moments of pure clarity and raw failure, which is often the case when bowhunting with traditional gear. I see an industry not so concerned with ethics but with make-it-easy approaches and savvy marketing driving bowhunting into new territory and, in most cases, one that has already been charted with rifles and scopes. Bowhunting with a stick and string is about experiences and a process that we all hope to result in bringing game to our tables. Those efforts take time to develop into formulae that connect us much more intimately to the game we pursue as we hunt closer.

That year it had been tough to get to hunt. I lived too far to get off work and drive to my family's farm to scout or hunt, and the few times I had been out were a write-off due to the weather. One evening on the way home from work, I ran into a co-worker of my wife who mentioned that he was heading up to his deer camp later that week. He invited me to deer hunt on his farm, and I gladly accepted as he lived only minutes from our home.

My deer season would consist of just three days that week in a new area I wasn't familiar with, so I had no knowledge of the deer that lived there. The area on his farm was small, only 30 huntable acres. In addition, a group had been hunting it hard prior to that week with archery gear with a week of shotgun hunting before that. I would have one afternoon to scout and two days to hunt.

I was surprised to learn the groups had not been successful even though they had hunted it hard, and several large bucks were frequenting the property. Even so, he assured me there was a high number of deer there. I met him the next day to go check out what the property had to offer. The landowner gave me the lay of the land. He explained that a large beaver pond at the back end was a natural barrier for his property, and the deer frequented an adjoining conifer stand for bedding.

I had only two hours of scouting time to put in and quickly found that the deer seemed to be using one main trail from the beds to large grain and soybean fields almost two kilometers away from the main run. They appeared to be making a loop back and forth to the feeding areas.

I found an area near the beaver pond with so many rubs and scrapes that it seemed that several bucks had been using it. On the way out, I came across two tree stands that the other folks had used on the property. They both showed frequent use and, of note, had been set right on a significant bedding area at the back end of the place; not a great idea when the wind was coming out of the north and blowing directly past the stand and ingress path.

Carefully backing out and taking great care to stay off the trails, I quietly left, choosing what I surmised to be the best spot for an ambush. Heading home to prep for the next two days of hunting, I was hopeful about what the following day would bring.

Standing outside my truck the following morning, cold, crisp autumn air filled my lungs, and it felt great to finally be out chasing deer. It was still dark, and the sun was not yet crawling out of the east to greet me as I placed my cased bow across the back of a small cedar fence post in the landowner's entrance. I could hear flights of ducks leaving the river nearby, heading to the same soybean fields across the way where I hoped to intercept a deer at daybreak.

I began to walk to the edge of the property, flushing three woodcocks simultaneously; the winnowing whistle of their wings contrasted sharply with the utter stillness of the morning. It was my grandfather's favorite upland bird, and I couldn't help but think it was his way of telling me he was walking with me that morning. Looking over my shoulder, I saw the first glimmers of orange peering from the clouds as I made my way to where I had decided to sit; a small berm overlooking the trail from the fields and 100 yards from where anyone else had been sitting given the location of the tree stands. I was on the ground but had 10 feet in elevation on the berm as it rose from an ancient white pine root, long deceased but still telling of its remarkable life. It would serve as a makeshift ground blind.

The sun rose, and the wind began to blow gently in my face; I had checked the wind several times as I walked in and the night before, and it was blowing direct to me. Morning hunts are meditative; watching the night leave and give way to light and the wildlife that inhabit both sides of the coin go about their lives is living education with a different story to tell each day.

I saw the ducks come up first, almost a mile and a half away; a massive skein of mallards and black ducks rising into the sky like a plume of smoke with a feathered soul. Something had jumped them, and several minutes later, I saw the cause of their feathered disturbance. He walked across the parallel fence farther down from where I had come in, like a king entering a throne room, the sun rising just for him.

The large-bodied buck jumped the fence across from me, still almost a mile out, and began to saunter towards a small broken cedar. I could see in the morning light that the cedar had many scars and was missing all the branches on its east side as the sun declared the massive rub like a raw wound to the tree. The buck walked up to the tree, turning his antlers from side to side as if picking a fight with the tree of life. Squaring up, he rubbed it gently for only a few seconds before attacking the tree with fervor and abandon. Pieces of the tree flew into the air, branches, bark, and mud dispersing for several feet. I took a deep breath. The buck looked like a donkey with antlers. As he moved away, leaving the tree swaying from his assault, I saw that he would likely walk right by my stand.

The deer followed the trail slowly, stopping to check the wind, and momentarily rubbed another tree en route to the fence in front of me. As he paused, I could see the husks of the soybeans he had consumed that morning on his jawline. Shaking myself loose from his sheer size, I began to focus on preparing for a shot. A shadow on the edge of his shoulder became evident as he closed the distance, and a stiff breeze blew his tail towards me. Stopping momentarily to rub yet another tree, he froze and stared to my left. Moving only my eyes, I observed he was clearly looking toward one of the tree stands on the opposite end of the meadow. He stopped there for almost 10 minutes, and I began to wonder if another hunter had entered the area that morning. Slowly he began to move again, stopping every few feet to scent-check the wind while staring toward the tree stand across the field. I had the bow up, pointing at him, and engaged live-string as he approached; the next few minutes happened without thought.

Focusing intensely on the line of his shoulder crease where his leg met his chest, when he stepped out across the eroded cedar fence and looked away, I sent the arrow to him with precise calm and exhaled. As the shaft reached him, he spun hard and mule-kicked into the air. I had been kneeling and stood as he ran full pelt directly to the thick beaver pond swale I had scouted the day before. I could see the arrow protruding from the ground with its blaze yellow cresting, now crimson, emphasized further by the sun fully rising in the sky as a signal of the events that had just transpired.

Hearing a loud crash of brush moments after he disappeared into the red and brown tangle of beaver cutover, I visually marked the last place I had seen him. Sitting down, and cradling my recurve across my lap, closed my eyes, and took some time to breathe. Almost 25 mins had elapsed from the moment I saw the deer to the shot. It had felt like several hours, and my heart was racing to acknowledge what my brain was telling it had just transpired. I stood quietly, listening, and gathering my thoughts.

I was aware at that moment that I had made my entire shot process before I even drew back the string, hit my anchor point, and sent the shaft on its way. I previsualized the entire scene in my mind. I walked to the arrow and knelt. The hit was evident, and I tagged the arrow and began to track to where I had last seen the large deer bolt from my view.

The tag alders were incredibly thick, which forced me to crawl to get through them. I soon found the trail he had taken. The blood started flowing almost immediately and was bright red and full of bubbles. I slowly stood as much as possible. The trail had become boggy due to the nearby beaver pond. As I stood to get a better view after crawling through the mess of tangles, I saw the expired buck lying on its side. The arrow had caught him where I was looking, through the top of the heart. He had covered less than 50 yards.

That day the Archer's Trinity became not just a process of shooting my bow but a honed method and application that had now become completely functional. It is much more than an intuitive process, connecting the brain and hand-eye coordination with kinaesthetic perception resulting in the ability to develop an instinctive method of shooting a bow. It is a process of self-development, focus, concentration, and training drills for hunting conditions. It allows for a progressive training evolution that follows: A Point-and-Shoot method in principle! Look, point, shoot or Bow arm, draw, anchor, release, and follow through.

Executing the perfect shot is applied by varying the pressures of the hunting process itself, then enabling your own platform, whether string walking, gap, point-on, instinctive, or even a compound with sights. That building foundation approach trains individuals to learn to shoot the best way that suits them and their chosen bow. I caution you on this journey; choose your foundation wisely. I see many folks considered internet experts on traditional bowhunting who have never pulled the string back on an animal. I am still learning and remain teachable.

The open mind absorbs information. The closed mind simply does not and, in many instances, rejects change. Training and shooting for groups at the same distance and target gets you good at that distance and target setup, but not necessarily at shots under bowhunting conditions.

Focus is paramount to executing an instinctive shot process. Without objective focus and concentration on your target, paper, foam or animal your mind will wander and so will your arrows downrange. Preparing to shoot will become a no-mind process; One that will allow you to index your bow to your hand naturally with confidence every time.

The tactile sensitivity required in the simple process of just holding and pointing the bow with an arrow nocked as one instrument tends to be where the brain begins to try to over-think the intuitive aspect of drawing and shooting at what you want to hit. Overthinking often causes overcomplication and distracting yourself with additional information will not help send your arrow to whatever it is you want to connect with.

There are three ways to do something, the right way, the wrong way and 1000 ways in between. Some folks, spend their entire lives exploring the 1000 ways in between, instead of putting in the reps and fight time, as soon as something doesn't work, they cast it away and try something else. Be objective with your shooting goals and understand that mental prep time is just as important as the kinetic side of being functional with a bow and arrow, regardless of what shooting method you prefer.

Find and focus on your right way, the journey of the *"1000"* ways begins with what makes your way work for you as an individual. The "1000" ways in between can be defined as your own journey and effort in the flight time you put into your shooting method, not someone else's.

Challenge your hunting abilities, not your distances, and I assure you that you will feel much better about the bowhunter you're becoming.

Remember, everyone misses. Count what you are doing right, not what you were doing wrong, this will help you stay present when sending arrows downrange and merge the instinctive hunter with the intuitive shooter, the final analysis that results in shooting traditional bows.

This path becomes the stepping-off point for the archer becoming a bowhunter, finding their own effective shot process and lethal range in the manner that suits them and the bow they are shooting. It is a never-ending process of self-improvement that will challenge you every time you pull back the string, and it will face your ego down at the same time. Find your own process, your path will ultimately lead you in the right direction. It is yours and no one else's.

Chapter Nine

Single String Small Game

Recipe for Archery Success

Traditional archery, from my point of reference, is all about bowhunting, not field archery or even 3D, both of which can assist one's shooting ability but bowhunting ability less so. The constraints in learning how to hunt with a stick and string are entirely up to the individual. When I speak of constraints, I am talking about the limits put on traditional bowhunting. There is much more than big game hunting to teach one how to manage those constraints. In fact, I urge folks to get youth out chasing small game versus larger animals when starting them out; it will anchor their interest.

Since I was young, I have had the good fortune to have a family that hunted small game frequently and pursued them with a bow. Rabbit, grouse, pheasant, and squirrels were abundant in my youth and provided far more opportunities; they have taught me more about being a bowhunter than big game ever has. I quickly learned as a kid that I never had to ask to take my bow out to hunt compared to asking to grab my over-and-under from the gun cabinet. Of course, my success rate dropped dramatically as a result. One afternoon with my Springer spaniel in tow, I missed at least nine times chasing a covey of Hungarian partridge for a half-hour. Emptying my quiver, picking up arrows, and trying again, spurred on by knocking tail feathers off one. I lost three arrows and never connected that day.

I recall sitting down, watching the setting sun, and staring at the two red feathers I'd knocked off one of the rusty grey birds in flight. I was so close but not connecting; I realized it was not impossible, and it spurred me to pursue the art and skillset I was developing. This development never ceases. Having that connection to our kit, bow, and our self-knowledge will enable you far more than you think it will.

Consider it your "woods" cred, and much like street credibility, or "the school of hard knocks," no pun intended, your path of shooting and hunting with a bow will become your greatest source of inspiration and teaching. The price to pay for all of this, of course, is that you will fail many more times than you will succeed on that path, but with patience and pressure comes self-reliance and a rock-hard resilience to match.

Several memories stand out, and teaching points to go along with those memories. When it comes to actual shooting skills, I have many that imprinted themselves upon my youth and left great impressions.

It was a cold day. A feverish pitch entered our house in late October, for it was my father's time to prepare to commune with the forest. Deer season had long gone, and back then, the archery-only season was a short three-week affair. Those days had passed; now the snow had come, and along with it, his second passion, which was to hunt and chase the snowshoe hare with his longbow. They were abundant around our home and provided many lessons to young eyes on shooting, stalking, and tracking them around the woods and fields of my youth. My father's rabbit stew was legendary, passed down from his father's recipe, an ancient blend of seasonings that were not allowed to be written down and had to be memorized to be recalled.

We met up with one of his best friends, a character of sorts and one that took hunting seriously with a bow and arrow. He shot the first Howard Hill longbow I had ever seen, an original Shultz-built "Big Five," a great beast at 70 inches in length and 80 pounds, its bamboo laminations sending the wood arrows he shot with absolute authority.

He was what some folks would call a snap shooter; he would come to full draw, hit his anchor point, and "snap." He was also one of the finest instinctive shots I ever witnessed!

That was it for him; very simple, and he was incredibly accurate at shooting his way. The whole crew at that time had nicknames, and he was "Frenchie." My father and Frenchie had a simple way to hunt snowshoes, paralleling each other around 25 yards apart. Walking slowly, if a rabbit appeared, they would whistle and take the shot; if the rabbit doubled back, then one of the two bowhunters would still get a shot. I was the flusher in the middle. We would walk into heavy cover, and out the hares would pop. Many shots were at running hares, and this day was no exception. I witnessed several amazing shots between my father and Frenchie that day. One stood out and burned itself into my mind. There was almost a half-foot of snow and was slightly overcast that afternoon. Tracks were everywhere. I was watching for the covey of Hungarian partridge that had made their harried tracks in and out of the field edge hours earlier, picking around for seeds and the frost burnt wild grapes that littered the area like tiny purple balloons.

I had chased them the prior fall with my young Springer, who was eager to see them spring from whatever cover they were hiding in. However, that was not to be as we stepped out of the long grass and grapevine tangles into the edge of the cedar cover and junipers scattered about. Hare sign was everywhere; tracks scurried all over the edges running in and out of the short but dense cover. I was already carrying two hares, one each from them both. As I stepped over deadfall, a large snowshoe burst ahead of us and ran into the open at breakneck speed. I glanced at Frenchie and watched him as he tracked the rabbit for at least 40 yards out, quartering and gaining ground. He brought the bow up, its bamboo limbs bending into a powerful "D" shape. Standing 10 yards from him, I watched the cedar shaft tipped with his favorite broadhead, a Zwicky Delta, come back to the stout bow's riser as he loosed the shaft. The rabbit was now in full stride at least 60 yards away. As the long-eared swamp bunny jumped a cedar fence, the arrow caught him in the air, and he tumbled to the snow on the opposite side of the old barren cedar planking. I was stunned for several moments after the shaft connected. I had watched some of my father's friends miss that same shot while hunting grouse when a cottontail or two would poke out of the field edges, and they missed with 12-gauge shotguns at 40 yards.

But this, watching that arrow and rabbit connect... I had been shooting since I was young by that point, but that shot was something else, on another level, and I wanted that skill too.

I asked him how he got that shot off. He said, "I point the bow, and the arrow goes where I look," then added, "don't overthink. I see the rabbit, what I see the arrow sees, what the arrow sees, the bow sees, too." He talked matter-of-factly, never missing a stride as he plucked the large hare from the snow and handed it to me. He walked away, pulling another cedar shaft from his back quiver, and continued onward as I ran to my father to tell him about the shot.

I spent my winters chasing snowshoes and cottontails all over the countryside, planning my day the night before, packing a lunch for the woods, and off for the entire day. I lost many arrows and wandered miles doing so; however, the cold never seemed to bite too deep or gnaw too hard as the trees hung low with snow and ice, and the world stood still for our Canadian winters. These things called to me, and I answered with stick, string, and determination.

During the late 80s, the terms "trad" or "traditional" bowhunting began to refer to and separate other forms of hunting to using a stick and string, be it recurve, longbow, or self-bow. I can appreciate why, although I tend to take a different stance on involving folks in shooting a stickbow. Simply put, anyone can do it, but it's also not for everyone.

I am reticent to go too deep into the weeds with these issues. I firmly believe that anyone can become adept enough to find a way that suits them to shoot well enough to hunt game with traditional equipment. The bigger issue lies within the very fabric of the weapon itself; it is arguably a skill that requires to some degree or another, consistency in its delivery system, and a perishable one at that.

As a kid, we had no cell phones or cameras at the ready. What I did have, however, were memories and events that became stories, which became legends in my mind; however small, or even by misfortune, they spoke to me as I grew and developed into some of the greatest lessons I have experienced. Arguably we all have the same skill set potential, but what sets some folks apart as "naturals," so to speak? Attributes. But wait, what am I referring to? The attributes are the physical, mental, kinesthetic, and kinetic skills that make techniques work.

Archery starts with the ability to draw the bow, bow weight, focus, concentration, intensity, and hand-eye coordination, which can be broken down even further in this development process. Now, the technical aspect of going through the entire process of holding, drawing, and releasing the bowstring is easy enough, but that skill transferred into dedicated and consistent accuracy is arguably a perishable skill.

So how do we get effective and maintain that skillset? By training and applying attribute development, training the skill sets that specifically make the techniques work for shooting.

I am so outspoken about the training development in shooting abilities directly related to actual bowhunting shots on game, and yes, ethics is a large part of the platform. I daresay the entire training method paradigm is centered around the very principle of ethics in bowhunting; not field archery, not Olympic style, or even 3D, only bowhunting specifically. How often have you been at a 3D range or tourney and said to yourself, "Wow, that target is too far, or it's in a poor shot position, or it's partially hidden behind a group of scrub or other obstruction?" We need to muckle onto what happens when the adrenaline dump occurs. Allow me to explain my rationale further.

When the sympathetic nervous system is engaged, we go to autopilot. When presented with stress, we default to our past, training, and previous exposure to the stressors or other stressful situations. We do not rise to the occasion but fall to the level of our training and flight time. In other words, experience with that specific stimulus or other related forms of stress. You will default to that level based on exposure, experiences, and, again, training. From my personal experience coaching and mentoring folks, this is the greatest culprit of the dreaded "target panic" issue. For new users coming from compounds, it is getting used to the bow becoming increasingly difficult to draw as the archer pulls the string to their draw length, which with compounds, will have been shorter. The "valley", where let-off occurs with a compound, is gone, and that leads to issues common to that very kinesthetic process where the brain expects to anticipate the break-over that occurs, and then the comfort of hitting the valley where a great deal of the draw weight of the bow lets off, enabling the archer to hold at full draw much longer in order to sight the target.

When shooting a traditional bow, the longer the hold at full draw, the harder it becomes to hold the weight of the bow; this causes many issues, the primary default being to lose focus and concentration, which is critical to shooting a stick bow without sights since the brain takes more time to "think" more on the process. The thinking brain is unreasonable under stress, for it removes natural reflexes, reaction time, and intuition. That would work fine and does, at times, on stationary targets such as bullseyes and 3D targets. Why? Because they do not move, they can't "jump" the string and the significant differentiator; there is no feedback from the animal.

Essentially the animal you are hunting is within a spatial relationship with you when it walks into view, and when it closes into proximity with you, the pressure mounts. Synapses fire faster, and decisions made; shot angles, vitals exposed, shoot-don't-shoot chatter, and for some, even the sight of a live animal is foreign to them. All these things become pressure, and without training in your shooting, no matter what type of platform or method you utilize, it will cause more failure than success and more shots to chance than confidence by not being prepared. That is not to say not those variables will not happen, but the more we train, we expose ourselves to the pressures of different types of variables. The more ability we will have to mitigate the problems mentioned above and thereby effectively deal with any other outliers if they do occur, and they will. It is hunting, not shooting.

To quote a very well-known traditional bowhunter I met as a kid after I asked him why he hadn't taken a shot at several bears that approached him during the hunt, he simply said, "The bear didn't give me the shot; he didn't present himself right." I have mulled that over for years and began to understand it after years of flight time and sitting quietly observing animals in the woods. It took time for me to be patient, focused, and have the intent and confidence in my equipment to know when the shot was coming, which is predictable to a degree.

The thing about shooting traditional bows is this; like a fine instrument, they will connect to you, and you will find your reasons to connect and develop your own "mojo" with that bow.

They have a spirit within that was enabled through their maker, the bowyer that crafted them. That spirit, though, is yours to find, and connect with. The merging of instinctive shooting and instinctive hunting comes from the same place, roots, and origins. The sparks of the past will ignite the fires of today.

Chapter Ten

Traditional Thunder Chicken

The Stickbow Challenge

The Spring weather had turned unseasonably warm as my truck turned down the long gravel lane that led to the farm. I watched as killdeer scampered ahead of the SUV, piping and twittering into the edges of the gravel with their trademark worried cries. I had been hunting the back end of the farm for two weeks, and it had been a comedy of errors. Two large cornfields surrounded the farm, encompassing almost 500 acres of land bordered at the far end by a small valley with a river surrounded by oak ridges and mature white pine and spruce trees.

There were a lot of birds; the small river valley was one large roost, and on any given morning, one could hear up to a dozen toms sounding off up and down the old irrigation system like some early morning, unhinged orchestra.

It was by any account an ideal habitat for wild turkeys; the only problem being along with many birds came many trespassers. For the past 20 or so years, I have been lucky enough to pursue eastern wild turkey with a stickbow here in Ontario and have been reasonably successful.

Our spring and fall seasons have provided what I believe to be some of the most challenging hunting I have ever done and, in some cases, more so than chasing whitetails with traditional bows.

Other hunters often ask me if I ever get a turkey with my bow, sometimes followed by a smart-alec remark or sarcasm. I often feel for that person who hasn't had the experience of trying to stalk a tom or draw on one as it struts into bow range without being seen to connect with one of these regal birds. From the moment the hen turkey lays an egg and incubates them until they hatch, just about every dang thing in the woods is trying to eat them. That they survive after the first few months is a testament to their wariness.

I have pursued and called them from hub blinds, from behind deadfalls, still-hunting, stalking, to finding & busting them with a pointing dog, then trying to call them again in the fall.

The birds can make a hunt seem easy one day and then make you feel like you're insane for even *thinking* of trying to hunt them the next: at times running in with abandon to a decoy setup, then scorning your subsequent attempts. They'll test your shooting abilities with a vital area roughly the size of a

tennis ball combined with avian motion, and they can run
and fly like a ninja out of a Sonny Chiba movie; there one
moment and gone the next. They will have you getting up
at three a.m. to catch the fly-down, only to stand you up on
the planned date and spin you around, gobbling back to you
to tease their presence and never show up after playing their
version of Marco Polo for hours.

The landowner had several issues with trespassers due to the
abundance of birds, and on one of the last hunts the previous
year, I helped the owner secure a fence and, two hours later,
finally secure his quarter horse mare that had run off after
someone had by driven over the fence, flattening it in the dark.
It had taken me almost two years of getting to know him to
gain access to the property. I had known the owner for some
time. He knew I hunted and had, from time to time, asked
for advice about varmints and such. As fate would have it,
he invited me to check out some coyote activity he had been
having.

I pulled in that day in early spring, and as we walked over
to check out some fresh coyote tracks, he noticed my bow case
sitting in the back seat of my truck. I opened the door and drew
the 62″ rosewood recurve from its case, paused, and strung the
bow for him to see. He immediately regaled me with stories
of his boy scout days and archery at his high school as a youth,
filling the next several minutes with memories. Moreso, he was

amused that I hunted with it for deer, turkey, and moose. By the end of the conversation, the topic of turkeys had come around, and he invited me to check out his farm, provided I used the bow solely.

It took some trial and error to connect with one of these birds. There were many showdowns, standoffs, and close calls until finally, after a day of hard work, lady luck shined on my efforts as I began to walk down the path to the old rusted Stelco fence that led to the farm lane. I needed to traverse the 20-minute walk to where I had hoped to catch a tom coming off the roost with my twelve-year-old son in tow the previous week. It had been a luckless day as the gate swung open, creaking, and whining like a drawbridge from an old Hitchcock radio show.

We had heard plenty of birds together and even had a tom at one point sneak in directly behind us, letting off a tremendous ode to our lone hen decoy for almost 30 minutes before returning the way he had come with a no-shot presentation.

After taking several practice shots with judo points at groups of small, worn, grey cedar fence post billets near the edge of the farm lane, and with my eyes warmed up, I checked my watch and was off. Latching the gate as quietly as I could and checking my gear, I walked over the rickety plank bridge where the runoff stream flowed west, cutting across the expanse of fields and fence lines. A pair of wood ducks jumped suddenly, squealing from their rest into the air and beating skyward in the sunlight like a pair of flying rainbows, then out of sight as they gained altitude across the large meadow.

I stopped as I reached the old barn, it was barren then, but its wood and straw odor reminded me of my youth. And as I took a breath, I carefully spied around the first field's edge. I was surprised, partly because I had been daydreaming on my way to hunt that day of coming upon a group of toms courting a hen near that barn, then making a stalk to get a shot. However, there was nothing; just the barn swallows twittering their displeasure at my proximity to their nests as they dove only feet from my head, chasing flies and twisting in the breeze.

Taking my binoculars, an ancient pair of Carl Zeiss I had used since I was young and using the old horse tie-post as a brace, I glassed the fields. That was not easy, for the fields were far from flat and had many small berms and wadis. The birds loved this terrain; collected rain provided water near the old waste grain and insects. I was wary of this, having once glassed for ten minutes only to stumble mere feet from a resting tom one day while trying to put the stalk on a different tom strutting two berms away.

I had time, as it was mid-afternoon and sunny, so I watched intently for several minutes before skirting the edge of the barn into the long grass bordering the first field. The barn was a stepping-off point for the hunt almost every time I was there, a key point of entry to the game about to be afoot, and so much more than an old horse stable and hay barn. Heralded forth by the barn swallow's intent on staying close to their wooded keep, I crouch-walked down the first berm and into the edge of the dried mud and soil next to the fence line. Turkey tracks were everywhere. "Raptors," I thought, chuckling at the name my kids called them when they saw those tracks as dinosaur prints and not poultry. When I informed my youngest that turkeys shared a similar hip bone with "Velociraptors," she was less than impressed and walked much closer into the dark woods with Dad after "turkeys" those early mornings.

The tracks were solid and hardened in the mud from the rain the day prior, and it appeared as though they were the only living thing on the farm that day as the prints littered the ground. I came to a small breach between the two fields and a connection point for the hardwoods that ran to the back of the property. That is where I wanted to be. I had planned this hunt all week and had foregone decoys, deciding instead to call from the edge of the entrance split, a transition area where I had frequently seen birds coming and going. I could see the back fence line and the first roost 100 yards away, yet I had enough back cover to break up my outline. Sitting under a small, low-hanging honeysuckle bush that blended into the old cedar post and rusted fence line, I cradled my recurve and nocked an arrow.

The sun was high. Usually, I would wake up two hours before sunrise and rush out to sneak in close to the roost areas in hopes of catching a bird, but the season closed in a week, and this would be the last shot at notching a tag for the season. After the bush behind me settled down, I took out a diaphragm call and made a few soft clucks followed by a purr. A hen responded immediately and paraded out into the field a short distance as if to say, "back off!" She putted loudly in my direction, then walked back across the dry, cracked field to the edge cover. As I watched pair of wood ducks I'd spooked circling back to their afternoon roost, movement up the fence line caught my eye. A jake stepped out, looking more like a black garbage bag shining in the sunlight than a bird. His head was up and searching the field rapidly. When I clucked at him, he stuck his head higher, then turned the way he'd been going, shook his wings out, and strolled off slowly down the fence line picking at the ground as he went. Several minutes later, another jake entered the field, then another, and soon, five more jakes were sneaking down the opposing fence line. I knew the path they were taking to the field and low ridge.

Late season can be frustrating, and these feathered ninjas were not making it easy. My attempts to call them resulted in some short raspy jake gobbles. They were interested not in heading my way but rather to the location where the hen had sounded off earlier. Checking my watch, I looked across the field and decided to attempt a stalk. After a quick assessment, I knew if I tried to cut back the way I came and head them off, they would see me at the main entrance for certain and hightail it out of the area. I opted to do the only thing I could; belly-crawl my way across and try to cut them off as the jakes entered the break created by a half-downed ancient maple tree toward the hen's location, an old clearcut meadow I'd tried to hunt in the past.

I began to crawl with my bow across the back of my forearms, slowly inching my way to a depression ahead of me. I'd then stop and look for another piece of ground to inchworm toward. For the next 15 minutes, I crawled through the mud and dirt, trying to keep my eyes on the birds as best I could while simultaneously scrabbling toward them. I planned to make it to the edge of the green stuff hoping the birds would not see me as I snuck behind them in the tall grass, then wait for them to cut downhill past me, where I would set the hasty ambush. I had made it almost 40 yards without being seen by the birds when a screeching cut the air from the hen's direction. Another hen had come out, and I could hear fighting purrs, putts, and cutting coming from the same direction. The jakes were now fully alert, heads straight up, picking up speed, and darting to the scene of the fight the way school kids run to a yard fight at recess. I could not believe it; I'd just spent the better part of an hour crawling toward these birds to have it suddenly end. I made it to a break in the fence line and crept through to the opposing side into the long, waist-high grass bordering the back end of the property.

I knelt and tried to relocate the jakes, only to see a swamp wren sternly staring at me from an elderberry bush only a few feet away, her vertical tail peak chastising my presence. I took a deep breath and heard what sounded like a hive of bees to my left and behind me. I heard the humming noise again. I came to my senses as if remembering some familiar song. I nocked an arrow, then tried looking over my left shoulder as slowly as possible. I was wearing minimal camo clothing, relying more on the cover than an older hoodie that I had touched up with permanent markers to try to bring some green out in the faded camo cloth for better concealment.

Slowly turning my head, I made out the tail fan of a strutting gobbler 60 yards away in the open meadow below. He was just off to the side of an old apple tree that had been beset with insects at some point in its life, with a few bits of greenery still clinging to its weary canopy.

In front of me, both hens had now entered the top of the ridge and were cutting up an awful noise. Three jakes were following them into the top end of the meadow 80 yards from the tom, who was displaying boldly for the hens as they continued their cacophony of fighting putts and purrs, taking false runs at each other. I turned back to focus on the tom who had seen four of the jakes enter the fray and stopped strutting to crane his neck to see them better. He came to a half strut and gobbled loudly, to which the jakes returned his challenge and slowed their approach.

By this time, I had turned my focus to the tom. I cut the distance to less than 50 yards by crawling on my knees through the grass. I was running out of cover; the grass was thinning, and the shade provided by the old broken maple was fading as well.

Now at this point, I was determined to get a shot on that bird. I had been training routinely for months for all sorts of shot presentations, sitting, kneeling, crouching, and had been shooting well. I had great confidence in the bow's ability to send that arrow where I was looking, but this was downhill at 50 yards, so I decided if I were to take a shot, it would be a headshot only.

The bird was simply moving too much. It was alert, not relaxed, and extremely fired up by the events. To make it even more of a problem, I would have to come to full draw with some clearance for the limbs in the grass and not be seen by the other five sets of eyes across the meadow while doing so. He was now moving to a low spot as he walked across the berm and down into the dip in the side of the ridge below, his neck still craning to see the commotion across from him. A warning putt sounded from one of the hens behind me, and I didn't bother to see if I was the cause. I rose slightly, fixating on the tom's head, and canting the bow for some ground clearance, began to draw. Halfway to full draw, he moved and dashed five to six feet in the direction of the other birds and then stopped, his head exposed above the green grass. I let down the draw; he stopped to look at one of the jakes closing the distance on him, the other jakes tagging along to catch some of the action.

That's it, I thought. He would be gone in a flash to avoid a beat-down by them. I rose again and came to half-draw, letting down a second time as he moved again and bobbed his head. Walking back to the berm with the apple tree, he again craned his neck to look for the jakes, who were now leading a collective section-charge to the tom down the side of the ridge.

At this point, I was still at live-string with tension on the red, black, and yellow Flemish twist string and once again began to draw, hit my anchor, and let the arrow go, never taking the focus off his head. As the arrow reached him, he suddenly vanished into the scrub where he was standing. I stood quickly, the jakes scattering as they and the hens sent warning clucks to every living creature within earshot. Standing slowly, I saw feathers float up from the tom's last position, followed by several wingbeats. More feathers flowed upward, mingling with the upper branches of what was left of the old, weathered apple tree and swirling into the forest beyond.

I approached, taking care not to trip in my excitement, took a deep breath, and as a precaution, nocked another broadhead-tipped arrow. There was no need. I approached, knelt, and admired his bold iridescent plumage. I marvelled at the difficulty I had just experienced; thankful the arrow had gone directly to where I had been looking.

I sat down on the edge of the small berm he had been strutting across directly under the apple tree. Across the top of what was left of the foliage, apple blossoms hung in the air.

Laying my back against the tree and my bow next to the tom, I sat for several minutes watching feathers rising through the old branches into the blue skies that had set the stage for the entire scene to unfold.

That year I trained weekly to prepare for some awkward stalking positions I had encountered while chasing these birds. The shot I took that day is also the farthest I have taken on game.

I get asked about my range restrictions quite a lot. It varies depending on the species and land I am hunting. I tend to be very picky when it comes to shot presentation on a turkey; the vitals are smaller, and the birds move around a lot and are very fast on their feet while reacting to movement. It comes down to what shot the bird gives me. I favor the head as a target unless the bird is very active and moving around like avian species tend to do. In that case, I'll shoot for the vitals.

I typically use a combo of flat face paper targets, 3D targets, and tennis balls – approximate to a turkey's vitals -- and will never shoot from the same position using the "one arrow at a time" principle I teach in the Archers Trinity Shooting Method. I do not want my brain to get content, and once I make the shot, I want to challenge my eyes and brain to re-adjust from another angle and shoot at a different target instead of chasing the arrow that made the last shot with another.

Remember, I'm not trying to score points or get a grouping. Again, foam does not move. At this point, I need to force the pressure onto my shot platform. Since there is no pressure from an actual bird, it's still sanitized practice to an extent. Sanitized means I'm comfortable, have time, control the narrative in the training, and haven't been sitting for hours in cold/hot weather, wind, or rain. Add pressure to your shooting! It will make you a better hunter, and in that process -- the keyword is *process*--you will synthesize the shooter and hunter into one. Don't get me wrong- I think it's great that some famous folks out there push limits on targets. While that's great for targets, it is not about distance. You show me a guy hitting foam at 70 yards at a stationary 3D target under sanitized conditions and comfort, and I'll show you the same fella missing on a live animal under pressure at the same distance.

Find the foundation that fits you, the individual. The long game in this process is the hunting part, being able to get closer. The short game is shooting so you are always hunt ready. Remember, "trad" bowhunting is self-competition, ultimately leading to self-knowledge. You will learn more by looking within through your personal experiences than by watching any canned hunting hero show.

Chapter Eleven

The Legend Of North Swamp

Antler Sharpens Iron

The connection to the animals we pursue is as ancient and old as our species. Conservation and stewardship come naturally for many hunters, as we abide by licensing, bag limits, and tag draws since all point to a process of wildlife management that hunters pay for each year. With that effort, we form a bond with the prey we seek.

As we strive to hunt the hard way within those diverse ecosystems, we become a part of the very lifecycles of those animals. Within this micro part of the process, we become both appreciative and protective simultaneously. Hunting with a stick and string is a continuous education, and I have found if you keep an open mind and a half-empty cup, such lessons will encroach upon your life continuously. Some lessons end in success, others failure, and as is the way of human nature, those failures tend to bend us to their will and sear themselves into our being as vivid cherished memories.

If you've bowhunted for any length of time, you know that sitting silently for hours immersed in inclement weather becomes meditative in its tedious process. When we open ourselves to that process, we receive remarkable moments to share with the game we pursue.

This connection to our past as hunter-gatherers brings our intentions to the forefront. It fuses us into the predatory nature of our species and the part we play in Mother Nature's Zen-like state of chaos as her wheel turns us to the ever-changing cycle at play in the wilderness.

This chapter is about an animal that served as a guide to me, more than I care to admit at times. An antlered professor whom I met on several occasions ended up honing my instincts as a bowhunter. Iron sharpens iron, as they say, and this animal's iron was cast on a different level, honing my process to a razor's edge.

By the time I first saw him, I was a seasoned hunter with a stick and string; I had taken whitetails, including some notable bucks. I have had other deer since that took my breath away, but he, well, he had something about him that was methodical and maybe included a lot of luck in his life. That something had kept him alive through ten years of rifle & archery seasons, at least one poaching attempt, and more than a few severe winters. He was on the cover of every outdoor fall magazine I had read as a kid, and at times he became a great teacher to me in the ways of the whitetail deer. He became known over the years as "The Legend of the North Swamp."

It had been a wet October, the whitetail archery season had been open for over a week, and there was barely time left before the annual gun hunt and the orange army that would be out after the same deer I was hunting. I had walked in later than I wanted, and the rainfall the night before had made the entire process of sneaking a soaking wet affair upon entering the old edge of red pine I was hunting in that year.

I loved this area; it was a transition zone of thick, red, tall pine bordering the back end of a large overgrown swamp and beaver pond. Tag alder and swamp maple persisted here along with the remnants of grey ash trees, many of them skeletal remains littering the area from a decimating ice storm years prior and an invasion of emerald ash borer beetles.

The cover several yards from where I was sitting was not fit for a tree stand; its tangles from storm carnage and many widow-makers served to ward off attempts at setting up in its darkened labyrinth of blowdowns. The deer loved it; food was plentiful with water nearby, offering protection and cover for bedding whitetails.

I had, however, found a good tree. You know, the one that calls out to you, with trails converging from all directions nearby. It offers good background cover and a prevailing wind that doesn't invade the bedding areas on your approach and restricts those sneaky swirling evening thermals that have spoiled many a hunt for us all. "This is the spot," it told me, "sit here, and you will meet success for certain." I managed to get into the stand that day without getting completely soaked.

The sun slowly rose as I climbed, taking care not to slip on the wet cogs of the tree while ascending to my perch. Once belted in, I carefully tugged my recurve up the tree to my seat. The full rut was not yet on, but the chase period was. I took out my small, handcrafted grunt call, which I have since sadly lost to the woods, and blew through it to clear the excess moisture while staring intently at a massive rub less than 15 feet away. As the sun rose higher, its rays revealed its actual size on the small pine tree scarred from whatever beast had made it. With the increasing light, it was growing larger by the minute. It was fresh and had not been present the day before. After I'd cleared the water out of the grunt call, I had barely stuffed it into the old wool pocket of my jacket when I heard hooves running behind me. Turning slowly as a slight breeze blew droplets of water onto my face, I saw a buck jogging directly to my tree from my six o'clock position. I barely had enough time to nock an arrow when he abruptly stopped.

He stood there and stared into the broken clearing I sat in. He was a stout-looking eight-point of around three years of age. He then walked carefully to my offside, where I had no shooting lane, checking the wind with his snout in the air. He then walked directly over to the massive rub.

Giving the rub a once over, he licked at the branch above it for a moment, then walked several yards behind the tree to a small blowdown and bedded down only 40 yards from me. He was in a good bit of cover, scent-checking the air every few minutes. He would stretch his neck over his back skyward as if appreciating the sun.

Several minutes later, I was distracted from watching him by the sound of running from the same trail he had come as a doe burst out and stopped only 15 feet away in the middle of one of my shooting lanes. I had no doe permit that year and watched her as she bristled her shoulder and guard hairs. Another buck burst from cover and ran at her; she bleated twice, then bolted. The second buck stopped short of the shooting lane, standing with his head held high. The first buck was now standing look-ing over at the intruder, a respectable nine point around the same age. He grunted in defiance and turned into the shooting lane as I leaned out to create some space to cant my recurve and prepare to shoot. My bow went up, and the arrow was on its way, disappearing into the muscled knots behind his shoulder as he sprang low and kicked into the air stopping only 40 yards away and turning to look back at what had just bitten him from the skies.

I looked for the arrow and caught it sticking into the dampened forest floor, shining crimson red in the sunrise and in stark contrast to the young seedling pines and glistening moss. The buck wobbled a moment and fell over, relaxing into the undergrowth and resting still in a matter of seconds. I slowly looked over at the first buck; he was standing for only a moment before slowly bedding back down and staring intently at the buck I had just arrowed. He then looked directly at me sitting in my stand, then back at the other deer, and didn't move.

I waited for almost 15 minutes as the rising sun fully cast shadows onto the beaver pond nearby. He turned his head as a pair of green-winged teal pitched into the water behind him, then looked again at me as if to gauge my reaction to their whistling wings and splash-down. Growing impatient at the work ahead, I lowered the bow, but he did not move or seem to see the motion. Slowly I descended the tree and, halfway down, looked over to see the bedded buck watching me as I climbed down. He stood as I hit the last step down to the ground and untied my bow from its hoist rope. Kneeling at the base of the tree, we watched each other for almost 10 minutes. He took several nervous steps toward me, holding his head up high and peering around the deadfall he was behind, then, as quickly as he came in, sauntered back the way he had come into the gloom of the old swamp. That was my first encounter with the buck that would become a legend to my family and the locals.

In his prime, he grew to immense proportions; a solid, large-bodied typical eight-point with some stickers here and there over time. I hunted him indirectly from year to year, and our encounters as the years went on never ended up with me getting a solid chance at him. He favored the darkness of the north end of the old swamp on our farm and was named "The Legend" for a good reason; he was the antlered king for many years in that area.

We had set up a trail camera to catch trespassers. One evening after dark, the camera captured a truck stopping across the entranceway with a crossbow and light out the window. The bolt must have missed by mere inches as they sped away. I made my way out the following day to check for fresh sign and found the bolt embedded into a nearby tree, a clean miss.

The local gun hunters spoke of him in awe for years, missing him several times on drives or running him with hounds and remarking how he always took the old "rock run" out of the adjoining swamp. They told me he always used the "heavy trails that ran into the swamp." Frankly, he used the tightest cover imaginable to escape their pursuits. I am always amazed how a large-bodied, antlered animal can navigate such thick cover.

I watched him one day, down the same road away from our property line, out sneak a group of blaze orange clad hunters setting up a drive into one of his favorite early-day haunts. I stopped my truck and watched them set up their push in a half-cut alfalfa field layered with brush. Their excited body language caused me to pause to watch the drive results unfold.

I saw his antlers; first, mere feet from the far-left hunter who walked past him while loading his shotgun, oblivious to his large presence nearby. He didn't move. After they had traversed the field into the nearby brush, he stood slowly, hunched down, and snuck quickly to the dirt road more like a cougar than a deer, then stood on the road staring at me for a moment as if to revel in his evasion of their efforts. I applauded him quietly as he vanished to the opposite side of the road.

Over the years, I had several failed attempts at him. Once he came to a stand I had painfully set in the middle of the mess and tangle of the swamp only to have him walk in behind me and stand under the tree with no shot. Another time I watched him walk to an old stand I used to practice shooting from. He tugged at the old haul rope, then tossed it around with his antlers only 12 feet below me before returning to the tangles he had emerged from. The following year we were allotted two tags, and less than a month later, I tagged out on a buck, leaving me with a doe permit. That day he gave me the only occasion for a viable shot at him, walking directly in front of my perch and stopping to feed on cedar branches downed by the recent heavy snow. I watched him bed down once again inside the shield of the nearby cedar trees. And once again, four years later, but at dark this time, he watched me climb down from my perch as if to wonder what the heck I was doing up in that tree.

The following year I saw him only once, and for the remainder of that season and winter wondered if he had outlived his luck. We saw no sign of him while hunting hares in the swamp that winter, where his usual winter patterns found him haunting the heavy cover of the cedars.

He appeared the following year, running through the small clearing I was hunting, chasing a rival mule-bodied six-point that was as big as he was. I watched from my stand in a tall oak as they brutally fought for dominance in the swamp inside the treeline 60 yards away.

He chased the interloper around me for over 10 minutes that evening, ensuring that the large six knew who the boss of that bedding area was. He hammered his rival with his antlers several times until, bawling loudly, the other buck ran from the area.

Apart from the fight I'd witnessed, he always appeared to be a cool customer, even during the rut. He had developed into a swamp ghost at almost eight years old, greying in color by mid-fall. He was still the topic of chatter among several nearby hunting camps and nonhunters alike.

He had great old tenacity and rarely strayed from secondary trails, paralleling other main runs used by his brethren. I once watched him trailing three does and a smaller buck as they made their way to my stand location, then watched as he let them all walk into it as if knowing what was about to beset them. I wondered if he knew I was there that day as he paused, skirted the back end of the fence line around me upwind, and began to feed in the field beside me as I watched through a thicket of hawthorn lining the fence.

That same year as he sat in his stand with his Howard Hill ASL in hand (a more lethal weapon held by my capable father, there never was), my father encountered him at close range and remarked that he dwarfed the three mature does he had been following.

"Saw the big guy tonight," he told me later that evening, "he's lucky," he remarked without talking much more about their encounter. Although without saying it, I saw my father admired the buck greatly, and I wondered if he had let him walk out of some higher intention that he wouldn't admit to me.

Another bowhunter and his son had allegedly loosed several shafts that same year as they sat in their tree hide, a large European gun hunting box blind they were using; they mentioned how he had walked over to the far edge after the last arrow had missed him, then bedded down to their rear 70 yards out of range and waited until dark before returning by their trail cam to continue his feast in safety.

The following year was hard on deer. After a harsh winter, I had not seen him, nor any of his telltale rubs and scrapes on the usual routes he tended to. I hadn't heard from any gun camps if they had taken him, nor had my local source of whitetail intel (the local country school bus driver) seen him coming and going. That would've been the first year I had not seen him yet, and the season was drawing to a close. I wondered if he had been taken by a poacher at night, hit by a car, or succumbed to old age. By my estimate, he would have been around nine to 10 years old, pushing it for his lifespan.

It was a challenging year to hunt late season. I missed getting a shot on a very nice buck the previous month. The buck had winded me as he came in downwind, circling to find the location of the grunt I was mimicking, and walked through a mess of tangles without offering a shot.

Being persistent, I braved a frigid -20 Celsius (-4 F) afternoon to sit near the old pond stand I once favored at the north end of the swamp. I had been watching two nice does that presented no decent shot, and it was growing dark. Behind me, a soft crunching in the snow warmed my senses, and I turned to see what it was. The sun was setting now, the warmth of the rays draining their heat as it grew darker. The remaining sunlight broke through parts of the cover as I watched The

Legend, still very much alive, slowly walking out of the same cover he had the first time I encountered him.

His gait had changed; his movement slowed by a noticeably slight, stiff limp and hunch on his left rear side as he picked his way toward me through the crystal white snow and prickly ash. His face and snout were white and grizzled, and his back appeared lowered with his belly. He raised his head slowly, checking the air, and grabbed a sprig of swamp maple, rolling it into his jawline as he walked and carefully chewed it. I had the bow up at this point and watched him walk through two shooting lanes, slowly edging closer to where I was sitting only 10 feet away. The does moved around us and back to the bedding area; I lowered my recurve and slowly sat down. I sat quietly as he fed around me for the better part of an hour, at times only 10 yards away as the sun hung low in the sky and faded into the smoke-like clouds, boiling with the promise of incoming snow.

His age showed clearly up close; he did not seem as alert and aware as he had in the past. He looked this way and that, his head bobbing slowly with each step, exposing his weary-look-ing ears, grey and grizzled jawline, and face. The slight snow that began to fall accumulated on his back and shoulders; his still impressive antlers were missing the left brow tine. It appeared to have been broken off in a fight. I mused he was still putting the boots to other bucks as best he could muster, as he appeared to have recent battle scars over his head and snout. He ambled about slowly and as was his trademark, walked behind the stand to my right and bedded down near the same berm I walked over years prior, only a few feet from where we had first encountered each other years before. I could see his chest rising and falling like a grey-haired mountain embossed against the white snow-laden ground. I marveled at that moment in his presence, considering what he had been through in his life, apart from what I had seen of him over the years. A reverence had formed in my mind that had always been there, but now stood fully connected in his presence.

It was almost dark now and soon past legal light as I slowly climbed down the tree and sat down at the base of the old pine; I could barely make out his shape, but his head was looking up in my direction. I stood quietly, beckoned to him by raising my bow, then internally said, "Thank you." His ears moved back and forth in recognition as if he understood my intent. Encasing my bow, I turned back and watched him rise carefully, still suspicious of my presence. He walked back down the trail with purpose, melting into the darkness of the winter with a slow gait, ambling into the bedding area. I found him the following spring as I looked for an arrow I'd lost shooting at a grouse earlier that fall. His skeleton curled up in a ball, head resting on his haunches.

He was lying in a spot where I had found a set of his sheds that I use for rattling antlers. I ran my hands over his antlers and skull, which showed signs of past battles fought over his lifetime. I have two sets of his sheds from his prime; the other I will give to our youngest daughter for her first set of rattling antlers this coming year as she enters her journey into traditional bow hunting. I sat next to him for almost an hour that morning, chatting off and on to myself and him, I suppose, about the harsh winters, and listened in silence to the sounds of his home I had hunted for over 25 years.

When I left, I carefully picked up his skull and antlers and marveled at them; even in death, he was remarkable. I noted his worn teeth, clear down to the bone. His lower jawbone told the tale of his life, an amazing feat for a whitetail buck in our northern climate and tremendous hunting pressure. A biologist with our fish and wildlife service estimated his age at almost 12 years. He had spent much of his life living in the dense tangles of that swamp, no doubt helping to ensure his survival.

I was then, and still am, very sure of myself in shot presentation. I've developed the shoot-don't-shoot mentality and instinctive shot process within my shooting platform that I teach to folks getting into hunting with stick and string. When unsure of a shot, I advise letting the animal walk rather than

162

THE CODE OF TRADITIONAL ARCHERY

wound it. If you're not sure, don't shoot! So what? The animal walks. Better luck next time.

What's the risk of a bad shot worth? The number one reason I have seen deer and other animals lost is not just due to anomalies and outliers; it happens. It is simply due to poor shot choice; the string should have never been released. Over the years I'd seen "The Legend," I'd been close to shooting, but the shot wasn't there, or there was too much cover in the way.

Last year while hunting for hours in sub-zero weather with my youngest, we had a beautiful buck come to the left of our ground set up. He was only 10 feet away at one point as he turned to chase another smaller buck away. I could've risked a chance shot at that deer, maybe having a small window to shoot an arrow through. It was not worth taking the chance; a low percentage shot often means a low probability of recovery. I let him walk. He came back minutes later, and we watched as he freshened a nearby scrape and licking branch my daughter had made earlier that year some distance away. Before leaving, he put on quite a show of tearing up the ground, grunting and huffing.

Back to The Legend; He was not the largest buck in the area, even though he was by any standards a specimen. Observing him over the years taught me more than by killing him.

Watching his behavior and tenacity, from scouting to setups and wind direction to shot presentation, he had fulfilled a role I still appreciate.

His skull and antlers sit on our wall now, both as a mark of respect as much as reverence for his life. He had shared with me as much as he could have in our predator/prey circle, and I daresay I was the one left feeling grateful. I did not just learn how to hunt his species more effectively, but in connecting with and hunting his turf over the years gained an appreciation for his hardships and habits while developing a fierceness in protecting the very wild places in which I pursue his species. I am forever grateful for his lessons.

Chapter Twelve

Through Her Eyes

A Hunter is Born

Involving our kids in the learning and having direct knowledge and responsibility in where at least some of their food comes from has been essential to raising them; from teaching them how to fish, with modern and improvised tackle, to foraging for what they have in wild greens, berries, nuts, and tubers. If memory serves me, I was learning to set traps, collect shoots, greens, and berries, build stickbows and fishing rods, and tie flies by the time I was six years old. It made sense that our kids would as well. Embracing the wilds should be a part of every child's rearing. In one form or another, it gives them a sense of respect and appreciation for their backyards as far more raw and real space than any classroom's sanitized learning environment.

I have come to appreciate how blessed I was to be raised in a family that hunted, fished, and foraged from the land where my family and relatives lived. As a result, I developed a deep sense of belonging in the woods, fields, and swamps in my formative years, which I now share with our kids. I feel much more content and safer in the wild than in any city I have lived or walked in. Watching them emerge into this connection has been humbling, as they are now walking, hunting, fishing, foraging, and finding their own path as individuals. I am learning from watching them, and I hope it gives them the same tenacity, perseverance, and resiliency in doing those things that make them self-sufficient as much as they have given me through the years.

Bowhunting has been fully embraced by our youngest now; she is learning the way of the arrow is not the path to instant success. The time it takes to be competent, maintain that competency in shooting, and get close enough to use a bow to hunt with has made its mark on her heart. I daresay the difficulty is 99% of the enjoyment and journey for her, setting all the pieces in motion and striving through the challenges that hunting with a traditional bow brings to her young life. Through this, she is becoming a better person, focused, driven, and able to tackle tasks with planning and insight, all attributes related to hunting the hard way.

I firmly believe that all youth should be taught to be intimately familiar with the woods in the areas they live near; to walk, endure, and thrive, not just survive in those wild spaces. Teaching kids that it's okay to be cold, a little hungry, and to be comfortable being uncomfortable in the wild is a good thing;

it develops heart and intestinal fortitude. Today, in a world of participation medals where everyone is a winner, more than ever, connecting kids to their environment, even occasionally, will center them in the true reality the world exists in that is now shielded from most youngsters' formal education in many modern educational streams.

The following story is one of the lessons learned from both father and daughter walking together, side by side. I hope she does the same with her children so that these ways are not lost to the plastic world spreading around us like a disease to Mother earth.

It was a quiet walk out that night, almost a half-mile trudge through six inches of snow to where my 10-year-old daughter and I had our ground blind situated.

She hadn't spoken much on the walk out, and as we got closer to the truck, she asked me to unlock the doors while she opened the liftgate. Finally, she spoke to me.

"Why, Dad? Why didn't you shoot?" I had sensed her frustration before we left the blind, and it had grown only an hour and a half later.

"I had no decent shot, dear," I said, trying to close the door on the issue. She jumped in the front seat and just sat there, cold and staring into the darkness of the pine trees as the moon crept through their branches, reflecting off the snow and sending dancing shadows on the bush trail in front of the truck. She looked older in that moment.

"I'm freezing my butt off out here, Dad."

She had never complained, I thought as we drove out onto the gravel road leading out of our property. She had asked to hold my hand as she had done on occasion while walking out in the dark for the past two years, and I could tell she was frustrated.

She quickly fell asleep on the way home. I went through the checklist several times since passing up the shot on the very large, and only, buck we had seen in almost two months of hunting. He was only 12 paces away at one point but only presented a head-on shot. He walked quickly through my only clear shooting lane, stood for a moment facing us, then disappeared into the gloom of the tight cedars as the light had faded, no doubt following the young doe that had run by us earlier that evening.

I knew exactly how she felt. It brought me back to my youth, being out with my father for hours in the cold. Her frustration was heartfelt for many reasons; the letdown and heart-wrenching feeling after hunting hard in the cold and snow for so many hours already. And I could tell her patience was wearing thin. I had been there where she was, just like anyone who hunts "the hard way" and knows what happens if you take low-percentage shots. Low percentage recoveries soon follow.

The weather had been harsh lately; we sat for hours in below zero temps, sneaking into our setup daily with great care to avoid the nearby bedding areas. I was firm that I wanted her first experiences to be self-learned teaching points, much the way I was raised. Bowhunting with a stick and string is challenging. Each moment we carry that recurve, longbow, or selfbow into the woods in the footsteps of cultures from all over the world who embraced that challenge for life and death going back thousands of years. It connects us all in its tedious unforgiving process. She was also connecting to this, to something more profound than taking an animal's life for food. I could see it growing in her, an understanding of what we were doing out in the woods hunting with a bow and arrow.

"We need to get back out there, Dad!" she exclaimed the following morning.

"I've got an idea," she replied. "I think we should move further down. We haven't checked closer to the bedding area in two weeks, and I bet the patterns changed."

"I'm happy you didn't try to shoot at him," she said as she explained her plan of moving our blind to an area closer to the main bedding area in the swamp edge we were hunting. Her perseverance was inspiring! We moved the ground blind, and less than a week later, we shared a memorable afternoon sit on the last day of our whitetail archery season.

On our way to the property, we saw several deer browsing along field edges, and she was very excited. A cold front had moved through, bringing a bright, sunny day. We snuck in and saw several fresh tracks of deer in the snow that had been browsing on swamp maple and cedars leading into the area we had set up.

After two years of hunting with me, she walked in the snow like a cat, pointing at each deer track shimmering like heart-shaped diamonds glistening in the snow, her face a large, creased smile as bright as the shining sun.

It was a long wait again. It was one of those utterly cold sunny days that generated gratitude for a warm house and waiting coffee. The sun had begun to hang low in the sky when branches broke directly behind us. The snapping branches sounded like gunshots in the crisp air. A group of deer was heading directly to our side from behind the blind. I balanced my recurve across my lap, looked over at her, and winked. A decent-sized 8-point stepped out at 30 yards and stared towards us, then one by one, a train of does walked by us only yards away until a lone large doe stepped out at 15 paces and stopped to grab a cedar bough. The string on the recurve sang, the shot was solid, and I knew she wouldn't go far.

I looked over at my daughter, and she whispered, "Did you get one?" "Yes," I said, containing my excitement, "we have a good hit." I waited even though I had heard the crash of the deer seconds after the shot. As much as I wanted to go straight to the deer, it was necessary to teach her that the process of the whole experience was what mattered more.

She checked her watch and, seeing that 30 mins had gone by, stared at me without making a sound with an urgency in her eyes. We found the arrow right away. I had her study it; the hair and blood left on it, the hair where broadhead entered the doe and the tracks of the deer as it ran.

Nervously she stepped forward with me as we traced the big doe's path into the thicket and found her piled up less than 30 yards from the shot.

"There she is!" she exclaimed, and we approached her together. We both knelt slowly, and she hugged me, then put her hands on the deer. She was speechless, looking both happy and sad simultaneously. At that moment, we connected. I watched her grow beyond her 10 years as she closed her eyes and said a prayer of thanks for the deer.

She stood as the work began to get the deer to the truck. We walked out that night in the dark, dragging the deer on the snow to the trail we walked in on. Our earlier tracks were already covered with a skiff of fresh snow. We said nothing to one another while we did so. We didn't have to. We loaded the deer into the truck with the rest of our gear, and as I looked over, she said, "Wow, that is a lot of work!"

"It is a lot dragging them out, isn't it?" I remarked.

"No, Dad," she said, "I meant the whole thing; getting ready in September, shooting practice all year, and scouting to finding a place to sit, too. All those cold days waiting! The whole thing is a lot of work!"

"Yes, it is," I thought, the whole process, not a product.

Several days later, while I watched her skinning out the doe, I realized the impact of what we had experienced together. She had learned in her second year with me how to scout, track, prepare, and, more importantly, be patient and develop a strong sense of resilience that only traditional bowhunting brings out as a true hunting process. She connected with an older part of herself, her ancestors, and the hunter-gatherers that came before us. We are not born of big box stores and parking lots; we are children of the wild, and I had felt it all over again, the familiar feeling I had in my youth, now through her eyes.

She has now stopped holding my hand on our walks out of the bush. She has a more profound understanding now and the confidence to match. Connecting to that ancient process is vital for us as traditional bowhunters and our children in today's world.

That was a first for her and me together that day, and this past year saw more firsts for her. For Christmas, she received her first hunting weight recurve bow, a 40lb recurve. She shot that bow all year and passed her Hunter Safety course in late

October. She scouted her own spot this year and set up a ground blind for herself. The first evening she sat for whitetails, she had a huge buck come in through her area but did not give her the shot she wanted due to brush. She made a good decision for where her skills are at, and I daresay I likely would not have shot either. That decision was already guided and tempered by her experience and knowledge. She is wise for her age. Many have asked me how she, at twelve years of age, can shoot a bow of that weight effectively and endure hunting in cold, miserable weather for hours. It starts with immersion, and that does not include making the outings something otherworldly, not at all. In other words, hunting with and shooting a traditional bow are all normal and routine; they are integrated into her life as a whole part of her upbringing.

The experiences and changes they bring are what make the process, her input, special. The same goes for her bow; she has been shooting a stickbow since she was two years old. She gradually increased weight and has been shooting a 30-pound bow for the past two years at her draw length, and as her draw length increased, so did the bow weight.

I will also point out that I allowed her to shoot without being overtly critical of her except for maintaining her form for safety and kinaesthetic development. Shooting should be fun.

It's essential as a priority when teaching kids to shoot that you let them go, learn good structure, and how to apply that to learn *their* way. Honestly, her ability to shoot is far better than mine was at her age; she is lethal with her bow to 20 yards, which is her current effective range. Working up to that bow weight took time and years of practice, but it was routine, not part-time. She is experiencing the results of her efforts now and continuing to improve her shooting and hunting skills.

Traditional bowhunting accompanied by bushcraft has become a part of her life, not a hobby but a challenging process that will no doubt evolve and grow as she does. We need resilient kids in this world. Take a kid hunting; it will change your world and theirs.

Acknowledgements

I have to give credit to my parents for encouraging writing and reading as a daily routine when I was young. They also allowed me to run free, hunting in the forests of my youth which gave me time to discover what was over the next hill without hindrance.

Jennifer, my wife has been a source of inspiration from the moment I first met her, a dedicated Police Officer and Mother. An adept archer and marksman herself, she has encouraged me to write and document traditional bowhunting for the past 20-plus years. She too was raised in a hunting and fishing family with deep connections to the wild.

I must thank my editor Jerry Gowins; Writing articles for Compton Traditional Bowhunters magazine, "A Walk in the woods" was an eye-opener; Jerry was not only patient with me but I was encouraged to pursue putting pen to paper, so to speak. I am sure I would have continued and stumbled quite a bit more often than I did without Jerry's support as a mentor and editor.

I cannot thank E. Don Thomas Jr enough for his forward in support of this book. I am humbled by his words, and I thank him for his years of inspirational writing. I have followed Don for the past 30 years. Not only have I gained much from his published works, but so has the entire sporting and hunting world.

We all, as part of the outdoors community, owe Don a debt of appreciation for being the voice for so many.

He is a leader in both ethics and conservation of traditional bowhunting, bird dogs, fly fishing and championing for our wild environment. I encourage you to seek out his writings.

Lastly, I want to acknowledge my youngest daughter, Indie. She began to follow in my footsteps at the age of 2. She took to shooting intuitively; so much so that it appeared she may have been born with a bow in her hands.

Waking long before sunrise, countless times, enduring rain, cold and snow with no complaints. Just being in the woods is good enough for her. Whether chasing ringnecks for miles hiking or sitting for hours in below-zero temperatures waiting for whitetails.

She is likely one of a handful of kids at her school who will ever experience their natural world and the reality of it in the way she is, she has made it her classroom. May she inspire other children to follow their own paths into the wild as much as she has inspired me, her Dad, to walk together in the forests of her youth. I am a better person for it.

About The Author

Grant Richardson is from Ontario Canada; He was raised in traditional bowhunting and bushcraft from a young age. He began shooting with a green glass longbow at the age of three and was shooting a hunting recurve by the age of 14.

Born into a family that has deep roots in both the bowhunting and fly-fishing community, he has bowhunted and fly fished across Canada and the U.S.

Grant has developed a unique method of shooting, specifically for bowhunting and instinctive archery. Based on pressure testing for hunting situations, he runs a mentoring program for those new to traditional bowhunting. Creating a fusion between principles of functional martial arts training and archery, the program is specifically geared toward people making the switch from a compound bow to traditional. He enjoys hunting and fly fishing with his children and working the family Weimaraners Ellie and Maggie on upland game.

Grant Richardson

Traditional Bowhunting Kit Tips

I am often asked about my set-up for hunting and how to tune arrows and what broadhead I use etc.

I am not going to say I am the first person to follow these principles, but these have served me well over the years. They are good benchmarks for the ethical use of a bow and arrow for hunting game.

I was raised around and influenced in the era of folks such as Glenn St Charles, Jim Dougherty, Doug Kittredge, Vic Boyer, Kiko Tovar and later G Fred. Asbell, Don Thomas, Paul Brunner and others.

Each one of these legends drew from some consistent equipment rules that allowed them to be successful and effective bowhunters regardless of what differences they had, the method they used to shoot, or what bow they preferred.

Here are some principles I base my setup on that have worked for me.

- Use the heaviest weight bow that **YOU** can shoot and **MANAGE COMFORTABLY**, with the

- **HEAVIEST ARROW** you can shoot off that bow to achieve good arrow flight.

- If you've come from shooting a compound bow, you will need to drop weight to be able to develop a good consistent shot. I recommend starting from 40-45lbs of draw weight no matter how heavy a wheel bow you have shot. In some cases lighter.

- It will take time to get used to the increased resistance of a stick bow as well as no "valley" or let off to hold it at full draw. This way your form will develop as well as the ability to become confident using a single-string bow for hunting game.

- Remember, hunting often requires wearing bulky clothing and sitting for long periods in cold wet weather, ensure you shoot wearing the same clothing/kit you're going to wear under adverse conditions or positions. Sanitized shooting is fine for maintenance, but shoot how you're going to hunt well ahead of the season.

- Achieve good arrow flight vs struggling for perfect FOC (front of center/forward of center) It is far more important to have an arrow fly well off your bow. Good arrow placement is what bowhunting is all about. A well-placed arrow shot from a bow of moderate hunting weight placed in the vitals of an animal will result in good recoveries. Shooting a heavier arrow also contributes to my next points on arrow speeds and having a quiet bow apart from having greater penetration capability over a lighter arrow.

- Speed- If speed is a concern for you with traditional bows, you may need to rethink some things. An average-weight modern recurve will generally throw out arrows around 170-175 FPS range. My fastest bow is a Howatt Hunter recurve, at my draw, it hits 63 lbs. Shooting a moderate-weight aluminum hunting arrow, I am getting around 190-195+ FPS out of that bow. All of my other recurves at the 50-55lb weight are anywhere from 170-180 FPS with a good clean consistent release. Now that may seem slow in comparison to some wheel bows nowadays. The big trade-off with the aforementioned arrow weight off a traditional weapon is a quiet bow. I would much prefer a quiet bow that shoots a good heavy arrow transferring all the stored energy from the limbs of the bow into that arrow. That accompanied by a good solid razor-sharp broadhead is what I am looking at for good penetration and bone-busting ability.

- Arrows- I have used Wood, Aluminum and Carbon. Arrows are as unique as bows; Find the one that best suits you and stick with it. I've used the same setup now for both aluminum and carbons for the past twenty years and haven't changed much. Why fix what's not broken?

- Broadheads- I tend to be fairly picky about broadheads; Having spent some considerable time in the past 30 years helping folks both recover and in some cases not recover the animal they hit has given me sobering clear objective insight into what makes a good broadhead, which is truly the working part of the lethality of an arrow.

1. I will use nothing but cut-on-contact broadheads

2. I prefer to self-sharpen and not use replacement blades- the fewer removable parts, the less failure is bound to happen.

3. I use both 2 and 3-blade heads, one for each hunting setup I have. They are kept surgery level sharp and I will accept nothing less.

4. Keep a spare unsharpened broadhead as a practice arrow for each of your hunting setups; Target points of the same weight as your broadheads are important but think about it for a moment. That broadhead has wings and dynamics that a target point does not. Ensure your broadheads are flying well before hunting

with them.

- Small game heads- Arrows are meant to kill by hemorrhaging, for small game such as cottontail rabbits or grouse, blunts and judo heads work well.

- For game such as varying hare and pheasants, geese and ducks which are larger, I highly recommend using broadheads solely.

- As with anything, safety is paramount- always know your backstop and beyond when shooting and hunting. I also use flu flu arrows for ariel hunting.

- Never use field/target points to hunt anything, it is unethical, and they are not meant for anything but targets.

Field Notes

Big Game Whitetail - Mule Deer - BlackTail - Sika - Fallow - Axis - Elk - Moose - Caribou - Pronghorn - Mountain Goat - Bighorn Sheep - Dall Sheep - Black Bear - Brown Bear

- **Mid-Sized & Small Game** Wild Pig - Javelina - Cottontail - Varying Hare - Jackrabbit - Squirrel - Ringneck Pheasant - Grouse - Quail - Doves - Duck - Geese

- **Food Sources**

- **Season**

- **Location/Area**

- **Weather**

- **Environment**

- **Terrain**

- **Wind Direction**

- **Coordinates**

- **Sunrise/Sunset**   **Moonrise/Moonset**

- **Date**   **Time**

Field Notes

Big Game Whitetail - Mule Deer - BlackTail - Sika - Fallow - Axis - Elk - Moose - Caribou - Pronghorn - Mountain Goat - Bighorn Sheep - Dall Sheep - Black Bear - Brown Bear

- **Mid-Sized & Small Game** Wild Pig - Javelina - Cottontail - Varying Hare - Jackrabbit - Squirrel - Ringneck Pheasant - Grouse - Quail - Doves - Duck - Geese

- **Food Sources**

- **Season**

- **Location/Area**

- **Weather**

- **Environment**

- **Terrain**

- **Wind Direction**

- **Coordinates**

- **Sunrise/Sunset**　　　　　**Moonrise/Moonset**

- **Date**　　　　**Time**

Field Notes

Big Game Whitetail - Mule Deer - BlackTail - Sika - Fallow - Axis - Elk - Moose - Caribou - Pronghorn - Mountain Goat - Bighorn Sheep - Dall Sheep - Black Bear - Brown Bear

- **Mid-Sized & Small Game** Wild Pig - Javelina - Cottontail - Varying Hare - Jackrabbit - Squirrel - Ringneck Pheasant - Grouse - Quail - Doves - Duck - Geese

- **Food Sources**

- **Season**

- **Location/Area**

- **Weather**

- **Environment**

- **Terrain**

- **Wind Direction**

- **Coordinates**

- **Sunrise/Sunset**   **Moonrise/Moonset**

- **Date**   **Time**

Field Notes

Big Game Whitetail - Mule Deer - BlackTail - Sika - Fallow - Axis - Elk - Moose - Caribou - Pronghorn - Mountain Goat - Bighorn Sheep - Dall Sheep - Black Bear - Brown Bear

- **Mid-Sized & Small Game** Wild Pig - Javelina - Cottontail - Varying Hare - Jackrabbit - Squirrel - Ringneck Pheasant - Grouse - Quail - Doves - Duck - Geese

- **Food Sources**

- **Season**

- **Location/Area**

- **Weather**

- **Environment**

- **Terrain**

- **Wind Direction**

- **Coordinates**

- **Sunrise/Sunset**   **Moonrise/Moonset**

- **Date**   **Time**

You can find our training courses at:

www.thecodeoftraditionalarchery.com

Courses:

Rapid Entry Into Traditional Archery

The Code of Traditional Archery Shooting Method

Hunt Accuracy Series

In-Person Training on shooting, scouting and tracking

Our choice in Bows...Damon Howatt Archery:

www.damonhowatt.com

Made in United States
North Haven, CT
09 July 2024

54566791R00125